The Complete Guide to

SOFT COATED WHEATEN TERRIERS

Gay Dunlap

LP Media Inc. Publishing
Text copyright © 2023 by LP Media Inc.
All rights reserved.

No part of this book may be reproduced or transmitted in any form or by any means, electronic or mechanical, including photocopying, recording, or by an information storage and retrieval system – except by a reviewer who may quote brief passages in a review to be printed in a magazine or newspaper – without permission in writing from the publisher. For information address LP Media Inc. Publishing, 1405 Kingsview Ln N, Plymouth, MN 55447

www.lpmedia.org

Publication Data

Gay Dunlap

The Complete Guide to Soft Coated Wheaten Terriers – First edition.

Summary: "Successfully raising a Soft Coated Wheaten Terrier from puppy to old age" Provided by publisher.

ISBN: 978-1-954288-77-5

[1. The Complete Guide to Soft Coated Wheaten Terriers– Non-Fiction] I. Title.

This book has been written with the published intent to provide accurate and authoritative information in regard to the subject matter included. While every reasonable precaution has been taken in preparation of this book the author and publisher expressly disclaim responsibility for any errors, omissions, or adverse effects arising from the use or application of the information contained inside. The techniques and suggestions are to be used at the reader's discretion and are not to be considered a substitute for professional veterinary care. If you suspect a medical problem with your dog, consult your veterinarian.

Design by Sorin Rădulescu

Cover Photo Credits:

Bottom Photo: Courtesy of **Gay Dunlap**

Top Left Photo: Courtesy of **Teddy Lei Photography**

Top Middle Photo: Courtesy of **Shutterstock/Wirestock Creators**

Top Right Photo: Courtesy of **Barry Rosen Photography**

Back Cover Author Photo: Courtesy of **Gay Dunlap**

First paperback edition, 2023

TABLE OF CONTENTS

Chapter One
History and Description 1

Origin and Place in Canine History 1

The Wheaten's Emergence from Ireland 4

Appearance...5

Temperament...10

Behavior 10

Chapter Two
Special Considerations..11

It's a Terrier—Not a Ball of Fluff..11

Care and Grooming 12

Early Training..13

Circumventing Behavioral Issues......................................18

Chapter Three
Buy or Adopt? Puppy or Adult? Male or Female? 19

Puppy or Adult?..19

Male or Female?..21

One or Two?..22

Buy or Adopt..22

Purchasing Through a Breeder 23

Purchasing through Adoption or Rescue..................28

What One Can Expect to Pay.....................................29

What to Expect of Your Wheaten Terrier 30

Chapter Four

Preparing For Your New Arrival..............................31

A Puppy Is not a Stocking Stuffer..............................33

Puppy-proofing Your Home and Yard.......................34

Creating a Safe Haven for Your Wheaten 37

Choosing a Veterinarian...39

Equipment Requirements..40

Chapter Five

Welcoming Your Wheaten Terrier..........................43

The Trip Home..43

The First Night 45

And The Next Morning 47

First Visit to the Vet...50

Chapter Six

Training..51

Housebreaking...51

Basic Commands 54

Walking on Lead...58

Physical and Mental Exercises.......................................59

The Importance of Early Socialization 61

Chapter Seven

Grooming 63

Why a Grooming Table? 66

Grooming Tools..67

Grooming the Wheaten Terrier...................................69

Bath Time..69

Nails, Ears, and Teeth, etc. 71

Complete Grooming Instructions 73

Professional Grooming Services 79

Chapter Eight

Socializing and Doggy Day Care 81

Socializing Your Wheaten with Other Dogs and Animals ...83

Socializing Your Wheaten with People and Children..........85

Puppy Socialization Classes.......................................87

Using a Professional Trainer 89

Canine Good Citizen (CGC) 90

Benefits of a Doggy Day Care Facility......................91

Dog Parks..93

The Dangers of Retractable Leashes.......................94

v

Chapter Nine

Dealing with Unwanted Behavior 95
Jumping 95
Chewing...97
Barking 98
Separation Anxiety... 100
Humping 103
Nipping and Mouthing 104
Noise Sensitivity 105

Chapter Ten

Your Wheaten's Health and Nutrition...................... 109
Health Disorders in Wheatens 109
SCWT Database 110
Nutrition.. 111
The Importance of Regular Veterinary Visits.................... 116
Pet Insurance.. 118

Chapter Eleven

Your Wheaten as a Show, Performance, or Therapy Dog 119
Show Dog/Breeding Stock 120
Performance Trials with Your Wheaten 123
Therapy Dog 129

Chapter Twelve

Your Aging Wheaten 131

Health in The Older Wheaten 132

Adjustments 134

Keeping the Mind Alive 137

When It's Time to Say Goodbye 138

Grieving 140

CHAPTER ONE

History and Description

Origin and Place in Canine History

If one were to travel back a few centuries to the Emerald Isle, peer through the Irish mist, and into the cottage of an Irish tenant farmer, one might easily find a rough-and-ready terrier-type dog—the poor farmer's answer to the handsome hunting dogs bred and owned by the aristocracy. Ownership of the latter, by virtue of stringent laws, was denied to the peasant class. In England, King Canute established the first Laws of the Forest, which applied to Ireland as well. Under these laws, only freemen and landowners were allowed to own dogs used for hunting, while peasants were only permitted dogs that were deemed incapable of killing large game.

The mists of Ireland seem to hold many mysteries, among them the true heritage of the Soft Coated Wheaten Terrier. It has often been said that the Irish are better storytellers than historians, and this may well be true. Suffice it to say, there is nary a book dealing with the history of the Irish terriers that does not use the words "buried in antiquity." One story has it that a blue dog, surviving a shipwreck after the defeat of the Spanish Armada, swam ashore off the coast of Ireland and bred with a native wheaten-colored bitch to produce the Irish Kerry Blue Terrier. This presupposes that the Wheaten was the progenitor of the Kerry. Early writings point toward this as well; however, one must also factor in the Irish Terrier.

In a nineteenth-century article, two Irish terriers from County Curragh are described as "high on leg, somewhat open in coat and wheaten in color." The writer goes on to say that the latter is what he "has always considered the proper shade for the jacket of an Irish Terrier." He writes, "Most of the earlier specimens were of this hue ... the bright red now, or recently, so fashionable being almost unknown." The "somewhat open in coat," descriptive of the typical Irish Wheaten Terrier coat, leads one to wonder if perhaps the writer was looking at a Wheaten Terrier and not an Irish at all. His reference to "high on leg" would indicate there were dogs considered low on leg as well. Enter yet another strain of Irish-bred terriers, one hailing from County Wicklow and named for the Glen of Imaal. This was a breed described as varying in color, mostly blue and tan, with an occasional wheaten and black and tan, long in body with "crooked legges," and thus more capable of going to ground for badger and fox. The Glen of Imaal Terriers were also kept for fighting other dogs in remote country districts, away from the watchful eye of the law, where wagering generally figured in.

These four terrier breeds, indigenous to Ireland for centuries, were collectively labeled "Irish Terriers" regardless of color, size, length of leg, etc. In other words, there were no distinct breeds or clear-cut demarcations among them; but rather, they were simply terriers bred by the poor tenant farmers in Ireland. It would follow, too, since the small villages were often isolated and scattered across the countryside, that breeding in those early days might best be described as haphazard. These dogs were not considered "pets" in the modern sense. Rather, they were kept as working animals, primarily to keep the cottages and farms vermin-free

and perhaps provide a supply of small game. It must be remembered that they were also valued for their courage and "gameness," i.e., their ability to hunt otters and to lure badgers from their dens.

It wasn't until the late 1800s, when dog shows came into being, that "Irish" terriers began to show themselves by name. Early entrants were described as "silver-haired" and "Irish Terriers (Blue)." So, we see that initially, the term "Irish Terrier" meant any terrier bred in Ireland. Anna Redlich, in her book *The Dogs of Ireland*, discusses the 1876 Belfast show, where "a dog called Slasher ... is described as a 'pure, old white Irish Terrier, a splendid field and water dog.'" Though the Wheaten Terrier dates back as far as the Kerry and Irish, it was the last of the three to be recognized as a breed by the Irish Kennel Club because its official name could not be agreed upon. It was not until 1934, due to the untiring efforts of one Dr. G.J. Pierse, that the name "Soft Coated Wheaten Terrier" was chosen and approved, and the breed placed on the Irish Kennel Club's official roster of recognized breeds.

As late as 1968, Irish-bred terriers, called Strong Terriers, were required to qualify for a Teastas Mor (Certificate of Gameness) to become Irish Kennel Club champions. The breeds involved included the Wheaten, the Kerry Blue, the Irish (Red), and the Glen of Imaal, along with the Bull Terrier and the Staffordshire. The Wheaten Terrier headed the top of the list, winning more certificates than the other breeds put together, thus proving its preeminence as a sporting terrier, excelling in "badger baiting."

As late as the early 1970s, Wheaten breeders traveling to Ireland from the U.S., this writer included, were introduced to dogs presented as Wheaten Terriers that looked nothing like ours. They appeared to have been crossbred with something akin to a Staffordshire Bull Terrier. These dogs gave the impression of having a tenacious fighting instinct, anxious for the kill. I saw them for myself, separately chained to doghouses a distance from the breeder's home. Another breeder from the U.S. was introduced to the same type of "Wheaten Terrier" in a Dublin parking lot. As a group, they were extremely broad-chested, with short, bowed legs, thick necks, and broad square heads with "laughing Staffy" muzzles and rosed ears. Thankfully, not all Wheaten Terrier breeders in Ireland strayed from breed type. Still, for a time, it took its toll on type and temperament since the gene pool depended upon the cooperation of both the serious breeders and those pejoratively referred to as "the Badger Boys."

Chapter One: History and Description

Photo Courtesy of Riley and Michelle Montes Capton

The Wheaten's Emergence from Ireland

By 1936, a Wheaten Terrier club had been formed in Ireland, and in 1943, the breed became eligible for registration in England. The early history of the breed in America has remained sketchy, but we do know two Wheaten Terriers, "Joyful Jessie" and "Fionn of Sona," arrived by boat on November 3, 1946, consigned to Miss Lydia Vogel of West Springfield, Massachusetts. The following year, these two were entered by Miss Vogel and shown in the Miscellaneous Class at Westminster. Although Miss Vogel continued to breed and show, most of her dogs were sold as pets and never registered. It was through Ireland's Maureen Holmes, considered to be the grand matriarch of the breed, that most Wheatens came to the U.S. from the Emerald Isle. It seems that Margaret O'Connor, of Brooklyn, N.Y., happened upon a picture of Lydia Vogel's dog, Fionn, in a paperback book, *The New Book of Dogs,* and it was through this connection that she ultimately reached Maureen. In 1957, the O'Connor family purchased their first Soft Coated Wheaten Terrier, Holmenock's Gramachree, directly from Maureen and dubbed her "Irish."

The O'Connors officially adopted "Gramachree" as their kennel name, and in 1961, Margaret showed Irish at the Staten Island Kennel Club show. It was the first time in 10 years that a Wheaten had been shown. The interest in Wheaten Terriers there was overwhelming, and Margaret was hooked! She discovered a few other East Coast Wheaten owners, among them Charles and Eileen Arnold (Cobalt/Sunset Hills), and adding them to her rather large Irish family, proceeded to gather the small group of dedicated Wheaten owners together. On March 17 (. Patrick's Day), 1962, they formed the Soft Coated Wheaten Terrier Club of America (SWTCA), at the same time creating the Soft Coated Wheaten Terrier stud book, a prerequisite for American Kennel Club (AKC) breed recognition. Less than 10 years later, more than 1,100 Wheatens were recorded. The stud book was subsequently presented to the AKC, and official recognition of the breed was granted on St. Patrick's Day, 1973.

Although a few Wheaten Terriers crossed the Irish Sea to England in 1939, none of their progeny were registered, and it was not until 1949 that the first dog show classes were offered there. The Soft Coated Wheaten Terrier Club of Great Britain was formed in 1955, thanks to the tireless efforts of Mrs. Corisande Read, who was well-established through her Binheath Wheatens. It should be mentioned here that Mrs. Read introduced a new dimension to the breed in the U.S. when she sold her Binheath Perro Benito to the Arnolds. The breed in England, however, was a slow starter, and it took 20 years to gain championship status there. It was not until the 1960s that the breed began to catch on in Sweden and Finland and then Holland and Germany in the mid-70s. While the greatest concentration of Wheaten Terriers is without doubt found in the United States, they can also be found in Canada, Australia, and, although in smaller numbers, almost every country on earth.

Appearance

The appearance of the Soft Coated Wheaten Terrier has a history of its own. When viewing very early photos of Ireland's three long-legged terrier breeds, irrespective of coat color, it's obvious that the three shared the same basic conformation. It was a bit down the road before they took on a look of their own. The Irish Terrier has a hard coat, a more streamlined shape, and small, high-set ears. The Kerry Blue not only set a distinct breed type earlier than the Wheaten but also established a distinctive, stylish trim from which it has not deviated. Certainly, the Kerry and the Wheaten share many similarities—for starters, both are square

Chapter One: History and Description

Photo Courtesy of Gay Dunlap

in outline and single-coated. From all reports, it was not unusual to find a wheaten-colored pup among Kerry litters and, similarly, a black pup in Wheaten litters. The Soft Coated Wheaten Terrier slowly evolved.

Today, one might easily be puzzled to hear "Irish Coat" versus "American Coat." To understand, we must look at the evolution of the Soft Coated Wheaten Terrier's appearance. The term "abundant" has been used to define a proper Wheaten Terrier coat since its earliest inception. The original standard of points, drawn up so many years ago in Ireland, lists as a penalizing point an "absence of abundant coat on any part." The Wheatens Maureen sent to America were of the Irish type. Their coats were silky, and they had rather thin (open) coats with soft and wavy or loosely curled hair of a clear wheaten hue. In the second generation, litters often included a pup with a thicker coat. They were quite appealing—the adorable fluffy puppy look. An early flyer designed by the newly formed American Wheaten Terrier club described the breed as *"the teddy-bear soft cuddly dog that children love to hug."* The same thing happened in the U.K., with English pups often sporting coats even heavier than those in the U.S. The latter gives one cause to wonder why the heavy coat has been dubbed "American," and, in truth, there is no plausible answer.

HELPFUL TIP
Soft Coated Wheaten Terrier Club of America (SCWTCA)

The Soft Coated Wheaten Terrier Club of America (SCWTCA) is this beautiful breed's American Kennel Club (AKC) parent club. This club was founded on St. Patrick's Day in 1962 and was officially recognized by the AKC in 1973, the same year the AKC recognized Soft Coated Wheaten Terriers as a breed. The SCWTCA maintains the breed standard for these terriers and strives to protect and preserve the breed. For more information about membership, research, or club publications, visit www.scwtca.org.

These "fluffy puppies" grew up, were shown, gained championships, were bred, and voila, a different strain of Wheaten Terriers evolved. Meanwhile, in its native country, the breed retained the original silky, thinner, more open coat. Mrs. Holmes accused both U.S. and British breeders of introducing other breeds into the gene pool. This was definitely not the case in the U.S. Early Wheaten breeders were, for starters, neophytes and, as such, also conformists. The mere hint of doing such a thing was anathema to them. Without a doubt, America's full-coated dogs were Soft Coated Wheaten Terriers of purebred Irish lineage. Some early breeders even questioned if perhaps Maureen had deliberately sent her "second string." After all, as Richard Beauchamp says in his iconic book *Solving the Mysteries of Breed Type*, "Anyone who has had experience with importing dogs sight unseen from foreign countries knows that the best of what a country has to offer is not always what is exported."

Certainly, and in retrospect, one can't help but wonder how the Wheaten Terrier would look today if these early breeders had not been so taken with the fluffy puppy look and had chosen instead to breed down from the more correct Irish-type coat. Unknown at the time was the fact that the thicker coat is brought about by a recessive gene.

Mrs. Holmes was adamant that the breed should be trimmed, but since she was speaking of the Irish coat, her view of trimming leaned more toward "top and tidy." She remarked that she did not want her dogs looking like "walking piles of hay." She was also adamant that the breed look like the terrier it was, not like, as she called the American version, "Soft

Chapter One: History and Description

White Nothings" and "Balloons of Fluff." It was not so much that Wheaten owners were opposed to trimming but rather that they didn't know how to trim them or, for that matter, where to even start. After all, no pattern had been established as had been done with both of its close cousins, the Kerry and the Irish. As a result, the earliest Wheaten Terrier standard presented to and accepted by the AKC stated, "The Wheaten Terrier is a natural dog and must so appear. Dogs that appear to be overly trimmed should be penalized. Coat on ears may be left natural or relieved of fringe to accent smallness ... For show purposes, the coat may be tidied up merely to present a neat outline but may not be clipped, plucked or stylized." Respected terrier specialist John Marvin, acting as advisor to the Soft Coated Wheaten Terrier Club of America's (SCWTCA's) newly formed Standard Committee, recommended the Wheaten ears carry long feathering, much like the Dandie Dinmont. The committee vetoed this suggestion.

The trimming issue did little to further the breed's stand as a terrier. At the same time, there existed a few powerful terrier men in the U.S., insisting that the Wheaten Terrier had no business joining the Terrier Group but rather belonged in the Non-Sporting Group. Their position, however, did not hold water, especially given that the Wheaten is considered the progenitor of two very well-defined terriers. The disdain for the breed held by these powerful old terrier men kept the breed in last place at dog shows, and it was many years before a Wheaten Terrier was regularly considered worthy of a Terrier Group placement.

In the early 1980s, breeder Marjorie Shoemaker put her scissors to work and, over the next few years, created a trim quite like what we see today in the show ring. Over the years, more simplified pet grooming techniques have been implemented for those who want the terrier look without such exacting constraints. Otherwise, the more full-coated Wheaten is destined to look like a little beige sheepdog, and the Irish-coated Wheaten will look like the scruffy terrier it is.

The typical Soft Coated Wheaten Terrier is a square, medium-sized, hardy, well-balanced sporting terrier. It is distinguished by its soft, silky, gently waving coat of warm wheaten color and steady disposition. The breed requires moderation in both structure and presentation with no exaggerations, presenting the overall appearance of an alert and happy animal, graceful, strong, and well-coordinated. Ideally, the adult male stands between 18 and 19 inches at the shoulder and weighs 35 to 40 pounds. His female counterpart is an inch shorter and should weigh between 30 and 35 pounds. The head is moderately long and rectangular in shape. The skull and foreface are equal in length, each a rectangle unto itself, clean and flat on the sides. The ears are small to medium in size, fold slightly above the skull, and point toward the ground rather than to the eye. The ears are important because they create terrier expression! The neck, head, and back are quite similar in length.

How the tail is set and carried is an important part of the dog's structure as it defines its "terrier-ness." That is, it should be set high, at right angles to the back, and carried gaily. A Wheaten that does not carry its tail up most of the time lacks the zest for life so typical of the breed. History tells us that the tail is docked and, indeed, the docked tail is preferred by most U.S. breeders. This is because most feel that the natural tail destroys the breed's preferred silhouette. There is a trend among some docked breeds to leave them in their natural state. It must be noted that the practice of tail docking has been outlawed in most countries, with the United States one of the last holdouts.

Pictured below is a correctly made and trimmed Wheaten Terrier.

Chapter One: History and Description

The finer prerequisites of the breed are readily available online at www.scwtca.org/breed/standard/.

Temperament

The temperament of a typical Wheaten Terrier is that of a happy, steady dog, alert and interested in its surroundings. Generally, the breed is not considered as aggressive as some of the other terrier breeds. But rest assured, a Wheaten Terrier is no powderpuff. He is loath to start a fight but will usually rise to the occasion if challenged. His tail can be a clear barometer of his intentions. A slowly wagging tail is a friendly tail. A quivering tail is generally a sign of insecurity or confusion and sends a clear message that aggressive behavior may take over.

Behavior

Much of the Wheaten Terrier's behavior depends upon early treatment and training, which is why it is important to seek a reputable, dedicated hobby breeder when considering the purchase of one. Training will be discussed in detail later in this book. Meanwhile, it's important to remember that a Wheaten Terrier puppy will ultimately reflect the behavioral traits its breeder and owner have taken the time and effort to instill in it.

The Wheaten is intrinsically a happy and enthusiastic dog. There are, however, a few behavioral traits that seem endemic to the breed. Their unbridled enthusiasm usually leads to the annoying habit of greeting people by ceaselessly jumping up on them. This same enthusiasm can manifest with nonstop barking to welcome guests at the door. Conversely, and under certain circumstances, they can show signs of wariness and need reassurance. These traits, as with all behavioral challenges, are modifiable.

CHAPTER TWO

Special Considerations

It's a Terrier—Not a Ball of Fluff

> "
>
> *Prior to selecting any breed of dog to incorporate into your lifestyle, it is of paramount importance to learn what the breed's original purpose is in order to determine whether it is the right fit for you. The Wheaten Terrier is not to be considered based on, for example, beauty or non-shedding qualities. Wheaten Terriers are very much more than this. They are demanding, a challenge, a lifestyle, a commitment.*
>
> SHARI BOYD
> *ARAN*
>
> "

Terriers are often instinctively labeled "terrierists." Following that, the Wheaten Terrier is generally thrown out of the mix because it is considered too gentle and soft-tempered to be counted as a true terrier. Neither of these is true. While one can certainly make a point that some terriers are feistier than others, most of them are alert, active, smart, and fun. These adjectives describe the Wheaten Terrier as well. Though such traits sound enchanting, they definitely require both owner involvement and owner supervision. What this means is that, as an owner, you cannot sit on your hands and leave a terrier puppy to its own devices, permit it to set its own rules, and allow it to run amuck. There is much to consider before taking on the responsibility of Wheaten Terrier ownership.

Care and Grooming

> *A nonnegotiable in owning a Wheaten Terrier is adhering to a strict and lifelong grooming regimen, regardless of the length of coat you keep on your dog.*
>
> SHARI BOYD
> *ARAN*

Wheatens are people dogs and are happiest when in your company. However, they are also den animals. The two are not mutually exclusive. It is for this reason that a special place, a den, preferably a crate, should be created. This will become the dog's safe haven for sleeping and eating. It will also provide an escape from the hustle and bustle of family life if and when the Wheaten feels the need. A good location might be the kitchen or family room, where the dog is part of the family but feels assured that he will be left alone in his den while there. More discussion on the benefits of a crate will be discussed later in this book.

The Wheaten owner who plans on a pup running around in an area loaded with weeds, leaves, and dry grass must understand that the pup's coat will be a magnet for all of it. But whether or not this is the plan, regular bathing and thorough brushing/combing are essential from puppyhood on. It is crucial that grooming begins at a very young age in order to ensure that the pup will both accept grooming and enjoy the process as an adult. Failure to do so leads not only to severe anxiety later on but also to a seriously matted coat, which will be both painful for the dog and exasperating for its owner. Keeping the dog's teeth and ears clean is also a requirement, as is keeping the toenails shortened. You must decide if these are chores that you are willing to handle on your own. If you aren't, you must decide if you can afford a monthly professional grooming service. If neither of these is within the realm of possibility, a Wheaten Terrier is probably not the breed for you.

Most dog breeds require physical and mental stimulation, and the Wheaten Terrier is no exception. This may take the form of daily walks on leash. It could also be vigorous tearing around a fenced-in area or repetitive chasing and retrieving a ball several times a day. Care must be taken, however, not to force a young puppy to exercise beyond its physical capability. For example, a two-mile run may be terrific for the owner but is too hard on a young pup's joints. The Wheaten will most certainly require increased physical exercise, incrementally, as it matures. A two-mile walk/run will be right up the dog's alley at maturity. Whereas Wheatens are not necessarily mental giants, they love to solve problems and learn tricks when challenged to do so. The mental stimulation such activities provide helps to create a keen sense of confidence in the psyche of the young Wheaten puppy.

Early Training

> *Early training does not start when you bring your new pup home, nor does it start at any one date on a calendar. It involves the most diligent of breeders knowing that early training begins with the proper care and environment provided to the dam of your pup. It is these careful breeders who pour themselves into making sure the dam of your pup is physically and mentally cared for before, during, and after having this litter.*
>
> SHARI BOYD
> *ARAN*

Chapter Two: Special Considerations

Training a puppy cannot begin soon enough. Wheaten Terriers are eager to learn and anxious to please. However, they need to be clear on exactly what is expected of them. If a puppy is not responding to its owner, chances are it is not grasping what is being asked of it. For example, confusion can arise when an owner decides inappropriate behavior is cute or funny rather than something that needs to be corrected and, later on, scolds the dog for the same behavior. This sends mixed messages to the puppy and fails to establish boundaries.

Setting clear-cut boundaries and expectations is essential for successful training. It also requires that the owner understand the importance of consistency and be willing to spend a few weeks totally immersed in the job at hand. For example, let's consider crate training. Unless you've bought a Wheaten from a breeder who has begun the crate training

Gay DUNLAP | The Complete Guide to Soft Coated Wheaten Terriers

Photo Courtesy of Gay Dunlap

Chapter Two: Special Considerations

process, it most likely will mean a few sleepless nights while your puppy cries to be let out of its crate, with you either ignoring it or stealing down the stairs to deal with it. "Dealing with it" does NOT include letting the puppy out! In all aspects of training, it is important that you win the battle.

Housebreaking is the most important step a new owner must take to ensure a long and happy life with any dog, and the Wheaten Terrier is no exception. Failure to accomplish this is the primary reason dogs end up in shelters. There are several choices relative to potty training, and they depend upon the situation. Training the puppy to potty outside is always preferred, but an interim choice might be paper training or the use of a pee pad, especially useful during inclement weather or with very young puppies. The latter methods are easily transferable by simply moving the paper or pee pad outside.

HISTORICAL FACT
Irish Farm Guardians

Soft Coated Wheaten Terriers can be traced back to County Kerry in Ireland, all the way to the 1700s. These loyal pups were the ideal farm dogs for poor tenant farmers in Ireland who were not legally allowed to own the more valuable hunting dogs, such as spaniels or hounds. As a result, the original Wheatens served as farm guardians, sheep herders, and vermin hunters and were sometimes referred to as the "poor man's Wolfhound."

It is amazing just how receptive the Wheaten pup is to training when the process is presented in a positive, fun-filled manner. Although young puppies tend to have a short attention span, they are capable of learning many simple commands, such as "sit" and "stay," as young as seven or eight weeks of age. The command "speak" can be taught early on as well. One clever owner actually taught his pup to do "quiet bark." Making it fun is the key to success.

If your Wheaten pup came from a responsible breeder, its early socialization has no doubt already begun. But it's now your responsibility to see that this crucial socialization process continues. Between the ages of six weeks to sixteen weeks, your Wheaten puppy's brain will develop exponentially, and this is the time period in his life that will be most impacted by experiences. Proper socialization ensures that your puppy will be exposed to as many facets of life as possible. It's a lot more than simply taking him to Home Depot! Socialization will be discussed in detail in Chapter 8.

Photo Courtesy of Eugene Lerner

Chapter Two: Special Considerations

Circumventing Behavioral Issues

Wheaten Terriers are prone to a few issues. Their proclivity for jumping up on people is so well documented that many breeders and owners point with pride to what has been coined the "Wheaten Greetin'!" Whereas some may find it endearing, most people are not particularly thrilled with being accosted by a leaping, bouncing, seemingly manic dog. Wheatens also tend to be overreactive to noise, which leads to excessive barking. A common complaint is that they go berserk at the ringing of the doorbell. Both traits are most often a result of the Wheaten's exuberant personality. The doorbell means company has arrived—and these dogs love company because it means the chance to bounce and jump for joy, unfortunately, often on the guests themselves! As with any unwanted behavior, both issues are easily circumvented with proper training and positive reinforcement.

One more issue worthy of mention is foot sensitivity. As a general rule, Wheatens do not like their feet touched. Since proper grooming includes not only nail trimming but the removal of the hair growing between the pads of the feet, it behooves the new Wheaten owner to accustom the puppy to having its feet touched regularly. Nail trimming and careful removal of hair between the pads should be done as early as possible. Responsible breeders generally begin the process of biweekly nail trimming in the first week following birth. Clipping the hair between the pads with blunt-nosed scissors is usually done for the first time at around one month of age. These procedures should be continued monthly, either by the new owner or by a professional groomer. Pups from puppy mills or backyard breeders are the most apt to display foot sensitivity since their feet have not, in most cases, been handled prior to placement in their new home.

The topics touched on here will be discussed in far more detail later. This is merely a prelude to what living with a Soft Coated Wheaten Terrier will entail if it is to be a success story. And it is my sincere hope that every story will be a success story!

CHAPTER THREE

Buy or Adopt?
Puppy or Adult?
Male or Female?

Unless one acts impulsively and buys a dog on a whim, the above are legitimate questions that any responsible person should carefully consider. Let's examine all possibilities, weighing the pros and cons of each.

Puppy or Adult?

> *When you buy a puppy, you are getting a blank slate. You can mold the puppy to adapt to your lifestyle and interests. When you get an adult dog, you need to realize he already has habits based on his prior life. He may be used to an urban setting or may be terrified of busy streets and loud noises. He may be used to small children or may be totally stressed by their quick movements and shrill voices. An adult dog needs time and patience to adapt to his new life with you. As you give him that time and make him feel secure, you'll both reap the rewards of a lifetime of companionship.*
>
> DEBORAH VAN DE VEN
> *Bradberry Soft-Coated Wheaten Terriers*

Chapter Three: Buy or Adopt? Puppy or Adult? Male or Female?

Who doesn't love a puppy? However, one must remember that, in the grand scheme of life, puppyhood is short-lived. On the plus side, puppies are malleable and moldable. They are, for the most part, what one might call a blank slate and have rarely developed habits that need correcting. Consequently, if one is willing to spend the time and energy required to train a young dog, a puppy may be a good idea.

In choosing to buy a dog, we often fail to consider the possibility of choosing an adult. When limiting the search to reputable hobby breeders, the chances of getting a quality, well-behaved adult dog are quite high. Understand that breeders keep what they deem to be the cream of the crop for breeding and show stock. But plans can go awry, minds are changed, or perhaps a dog is shown and then placed as a pet. Sometimes, a lovely female is bred and then spayed before being placed in a pet home. Hobby breeders can't keep everything; room must be made for new stock.

The thoughtful breeder appreciates that a dog is happiest when in a home where it may be treated as "an only child" rather than one of many. These dogs have been raised by an expert and given the best start in life. Many have had significant training and are accustomed to grooming and traveling as well. A reputable hobby breeder will always place an adult dog conditionally; this means the placement is with the understanding that the new owner must return the dog if, for any reason, the relationship is not a pleasing one for both the new owner and dog. Most breeders do not openly advertise adult dogs, so it is well worth inquiring.

Male or Female?

> *People often have a preference for a boy or girl dog based on the dogs they've known in their lifetime. Boy Wheatens tend to be super sweet, devoted companions. Girl Wheatens can be slightly more independent than boys, but in my experience are also very affectionate and loyal. Remember, every dog is an individual. Your new puppy will have his own personality and might be very different from your previous dog. That's what makes them so special and unique. Wheatens generally love the company of a second dog in their home. This is usually most successful with one dog of each sex, rather than two boys or two girls. It is also important that the first dog is very dog friendly and still young enough to welcome the exuberance and antics of a puppy sibling.*
>
> DEBORAH VAN DE VEN
> *Bradberry Soft-Coated Wheaten Terriers*

The delightful experience of owning a Wheaten male dog is often lost due to the general belief that males have objectionable habits, such as lifting their leg in the house and indiscriminate humping. As has been said before, such habits are easily breakable with training. It is also thought that females are more docile and sweet, while the boys tend to be rough and tumble. However, many breeders will tell you that if they could only have one Wheaten Terrier, it would be a boy. Wheaten Terrier boys are generally loving and deeply loyal to their owners, while the girls tend to be somewhat fickle and love the person they are with at the moment, whoever that may be! In truth, neutering or spaying generally places both genders on an even scale behaviorally. Neutering a male is less costly than spaying a female, and the recovery time is faster, too.

Chapter Three: Buy or Adopt? Puppy or Adult? Male or Female?

One or Two?

> *Your prior experience in owning dogs should and will play a part in which sex of pup best fits your lifestyle. When working with a reputable breeder, a prospective family can expect a pup to be chosen for them. A pup takes a lot of work to properly and successfully raise. Rarely will a reputable breeder place more than one pup at a time with a family.*
>
> SHARI BOYD
> *ARAN*

Raising two puppies together can be a difficult task. In fact, many reputable breeders will refuse to sell two puppies from the same litter at the same time. The primary reason for this is that the puppies will tend to bond with each other rather than with their new family. This, in turn, can cause interaction with their new family to be adversely affected. Training two puppies simultaneously will be challenging, but with extra time and effort, it can be done. It's recommended that one dog of each gender be chosen since same-sex puppies may end up fighting with each other at maturity. Firm boundaries and early intervention are key. On the plus side, two puppies often adjust to their new environment much faster and keep each other exercised and entertained.

Buy or Adopt

The choice of buying versus adopting, unfortunately, has become somewhat contentious and often emotionally charged. If we look at the choice objectively, we find there are pros and cons to each.

Purchasing Through a Breeder

The advantages of buying from a breeder, assuming it is a reputable one, are many. The sire of your Wheaten will have been carefully chosen to maximize positive physical and emotional traits. Generally, the puppy's parents will be AKC Champions of Record. They will have been health tested and certified free of genetic disease. You may also find that the puppy has received some early crate training. Most importantly, the serious hobby breeder will be there throughout the life of your Wheaten Terrier, becoming your best source of accurate information concerning your dog.

The primary disadvantage to buying your Wheaten puppy from a breeder is financial. The expenses incurred by a serious hobby breeder in order to offer healthy, thoughtfully bred pups are imposing, starting with the stud fee. One must also factor in the cost of all testing, certifications, early inoculations, registrations, and veterinary fees. Consequently, prices for the resulting puppies are designed to offset these expenses.

Another aspect of buying from a breeder that might be considered a disadvantage is the research required to distinguish a responsible,

Chapter Three: Buy or Adopt? Puppy or Adult? Male or Female?

quality breeder from backyard breeders or puppy mills. Sadly, there are many irresponsible breeders out there. The best way to locate reputable breeders is to contact the breed's national breed club, in this instance, the SCWTCA. The club's website offers a list of breeders by state. There are also local Wheaten Terrier clubs scattered across the country, and some of these have websites as well.

Photo Courtesy of Gay Dunlap

Finding a Reputable Breeder and What to Expect

> *I strongly recommend research into more than just the closest breeder geographically. Interview breeders as you would a childcare worker. Understand what questions you should ask and why you are asking them. Given the ease of gathering information these days, read, read, read. Above all, ask your potential breeder what testing they do. If the answer doesn't match the list on the National Wheaten Club's health tests, thank them and continue your search elsewhere. Ask if, for any reason, you cannot keep the puppy at any point in its life, will the breeder take the pup/adult back. If the answer is not a quick yes, thank them and continue your search elsewhere. There will always be another litter of puppies coming up. Be diligent, ask the tough questions, and do your due diligence; the rewards will be the well-bred, well-socialized puppy you get to bring home.*
>
> **SHARI ROBINSON**
> *Keepsake Wheatens*

As mentioned earlier, the most effective way to locate dedicated, reputable breeders is through a national breed club website. This is true for all purebred dogs, not just the Soft-Coated Wheaten Terrier. The Wheaten Terrier national breed club's website address is https://www.scwtca.org. There, one will find breeders listed by state.

Before going further, it's important to understand exactly what the term "AKC Registered" means. It means that the dog is purebred and only that. It does not imply well bred, thoughtfully bred, or bred for the preservation of the breed. Any two dogs of the same breed, regardless of quality, can mate and qualify for AKC registration. This is an important distinction since many people have the mistaken idea that because

Chapter Three: Buy or Adopt? Puppy or Adult? Male or Female?

a puppy is "AKC registered," it will also be carefully bred by a reputable breeder. This is not the case. Just because someone breeds two dogs to make puppies does not make them a reputable breeder.

A reputable breeder is someone who puts the quality, health, and welfare of their dogs first. Conversely, backyard or puppy mill breeders put monetary gain ahead of their dogs' health and well-being. In the process, the decisions they make often adversely affect their dogs' future. Although many people buy dogs through the latter source, it is a bad route to follow since irresponsibly bred dogs are far more likely to have serious health and temperament problems, making for deeply frustrating and ultimately heartbreaking experiences. These breeders continue to exist because uninformed people buy puppies from them. If this weren't the case, backyard and puppy mill breeders would cease to be in business.

Reputable breeders do not consider themselves to be "in business." It is their passion, and they are dedicated to the preservation of their respective breeds. Additionally, reputable breeders who are members of their national club have pledged to abide by a strict code of ethics. This is certainly true of Soft-Coated Wheaten Terrier breeders who belong to SCWTCA, Inc. It may also be true of those who belong to local specialty breed clubs. Serious, dedicated breeders show their dogs at AKC-licensed conformation events, gaining championship titles on them prior to their use as breeding stock. These events are designed to prove the worth of breeding stock, and adding a championship title indicates that the sire and dam of your puppy conform to the breed's standard of excellence.

Another avenue for identifying dedicated reputable breeders is the online SCWTCA database at http://www.scwtdb.org. If you want information about a specific breeder, go to the website and click on "Database" to enter. Then click on "People" and enter the breeder's last name. If the breeder does not show up, it means they are not health testing their dogs.

Reputable breeders do not have puppies available on a regular basis, which is another way to distinguish dedicated breeders from others. They will generally have, at most, a couple of litters a year, so you may have to agree to go on a waiting list. These breeders generally support one another and are happy to suggest other breeders that either have puppies available or are expecting them soon.

Reputable breeders will want to interview you in order to feel confident that you are the sort of owner they feel will give a puppy a good home. At the same time, breeders will expect you to ask the right questions, proving that you understand the commitment involved in taking a puppy home. For example, you will want to ask about the genetic and health screening done on their breeding stock, especially the sire and dam of the puppy. Your knowledge regarding the importance of such testing will send a clear message about the level of your expectations. Breeders should be happy to set a date for you to meet their dogs and see how they are kept. Are they clean and healthy? Are they kept in a clean environment? Are they accepting and friendly, or do they appear to be skittish or aggressive? If a breeder can't be visited because of distance, can they provide references from other buyers? Steer clear of a breeder who refuses to allow you to visit or seems to have a hidden agenda.

Health Testing and Certifications

Reputable breeders should provide proof that the sire and dam are free of hip dysplasia and that their eyes have been examined by a veterinarian ophthalmologist for genetic defects. These tests are mandatory for SCWTCA breeders/members to remain in good standing with the club. Another requirement mandates that only dogs over a specific age be used as breeding stock. All health testing protocols, either suggested or mandated by the club, can be viewed at www.scwtca.org/the-club/code-of-ethics. If the puppy is being sold as a pet (not for show or breeding stock), one can expect to contractually agree that it will be neutered at a recommended age. Included in this contract will be your commitment to perform yearly health testing protocols, along with a requirement that the dog be returned to the breeder if, for any reason, it must be placed. The conscientious breeder will ask to be kept informed of any problems that may arise, regardless of the dog's age. Your relationship with the reputable breeder should be for the life of the dog. Walk away from any breeder who is reluctant to discuss health issues or downplays the importance of health testing.

Chapter Three: Buy or Adopt? Puppy or Adult? Male or Female?

Purchasing through Adoption or Rescue

What are the advantages of adopting? A Wheaten Terrier obtained through rescue or a shelter can be bought at a fraction of what it would cost from a breeder and is most often already spayed or neutered. It will also be up to date with its veterinary care and vaccinations. Then there is also the "feel good" state this act of compassion leaves us with when we provide a forever home for a Wheaten Terrier that has none.

One must realize, however, that virtually no reputably bred Wheaten Terrier ends up in rescue. This is because responsible breeders contractually require that a dog bred by them be returned to them if, for any reason, it can't be kept by its owner. This means that most, if not all, rescue Wheaten Terriers are from backyard breeders or puppy mills. Therefore, it is doubtful that a rescue Wheaten has been health tested or received hip/eye certification. The same would hold true for its sire and dam. Consequently, dogs sourced in this manner are far more apt to have health and/or temperament problems.

When choosing a Wheaten from an all-breed shelter, odds are great that the dog being introduced to you is not a Soft Coated Wheaten Terrier. Shelter people often guess regarding a dog's lineage and base their claim on little more than conjecture. Remember, there's a reason these dogs were brought into the shelter in

HELPFUL TIP
Choosing a Wheaten Rescue

If you decide to rescue a Wheaten, you'll want to start looking into reputable shelters or rescues. Breed-specific rescues are available for many dog breeds, including Soft Coated Wheaten Terriers. Two such breed-specific organizations in North America are National Wheaten Rescue, Inc. (NWR) and and Wheaten's In Need (WIN), both of which are registered 501(c)3 nonprofits. In partnership with the SCWTCA, the NWR rescued or rehomed 1,767 purebred Wheaten terriers between 1993 and 2020. For more information about these rescues, visit www.nationalwheatenrescueinc.org and https://wheatensinneed.org/.

the first place. As a result, they may require additional training, patience, and empathy from you as they adjust to their new home and surroundings. One way to ensure that you are getting a bona fide Soft Coated Wheaten Terrier is through the two purebred Wheaten Terrier rescue programs, Wheatens In Need and National Wheaten Rescue. Both are IRS 501(c)3 tax-exempt organizations.

Whereas DNA testing is available to establish a dog's lineage, at this writing, there are veterinarians and genetic experts as yet unwilling to stamp these kits with a seal of accuracy. Although anecdotal evidence suggests that many dog owners believe the DNA kits are generally accurate—citing the kits' accuracy in identifying information that dog owners can confirm, such as hair color and, in some cases, breed—there isn't verifiable, third-party data to corroborate the information. This doesn't necessarily mean that DNA test kits for your dog are a waste of money or that they're likely to provide wrong information, but dog owners should take results with a grain of salt. Even in the best-case scenario, these tests have the potential to be wrong. Still, it is quite possible that such a test can help the new owners of a shelter Wheaten learn valuable information to improve their ability to give their dog the support, care, and medical attention it needs to live a long, happy life.

What One Can Expect to Pay

Price Through Rescue/Adoption

Whereas rescue or adoption of a Soft Coated Wheaten Terrier costs a fraction of what one might pay for a dog purchased from a respected hobby breeder, there will be a fee. The fee offsets the many expenses incurred to ensure that your rescue dog is healthy, free from disease, and emotionally stable. At this writing, rescue or adoption fees range from $300 to $500, plus the expense of a crate and shipping costs.

Chapter Three: Buy or Adopt? Puppy or Adult? Male or Female?

Price Through Breeder

The cost of a Wheaten puppy from a reputable breeder is usually commensurate with the cost of the stud fee, and stud fees can run from $2,500 to $4,000. In addition to the stud fee, there are veterinary bills incurred in maintaining the health of the dam and puppies. These expenses, along with the cost of various registrations, certifications, and health testing, add up. There is something else worth mentioning here, and that is, if time equals money, responsible breeders work for peanuts. Breeding purposefully and thoughtfully requires a passion that knows no bounds, and in truth, there are few, if any, reputable breeders that consider what they do to be a money-making proposition. In fact, they seldom break even. If ever there was a labor of love, this is it.

What to Expect of Your Wheaten Terrier

If your Wheaten was brought into the world by a reputable breeder and you have done due diligence, you can expect that it will be good with children. Its projected behavior with other established pets depends upon the pet, so this is a question best put to the breeder. Remember that it is a terrier and, upon maturity, may not be particularly welcoming of tiny animals. You should be able to assume you will not be plagued with health problems and that your dog will provide you with years of loving companionship. Well-bred Wheaten Terriers generally have a life span of between 12 and 15 years, with a few living beyond. Unfortunately, the same does not always hold true with Wheatens from backyard breeders or those bred in puppy mills.

Photo Courtesy of Gay Dunlap

CHAPTER FOUR

Preparing For Your New Arrival

> *Soft-Coated Wheaten Terriers are amazing pets but require consistent coat care and training. They are wonderful with children, with the elderly, with people who work full time, and with stay-at-home folks. They are equally at home in a Fifth Avenue apartment as they are in the country. Training and exercise are the key. A Wheaten is very intelligent and will work with you or devise ways to outsmart you. It is their version of Terrier games. Charming, manipulative, funny, joyful, and so very sweet ... They are great for everyone, but everyone is not great for them.Trust your breeder to choose a pup that will fit your lifestyle, and expect a thorough interview because a thoughtful breeder wants what is best for the puppy and for your family!*
>
> EMILY HOLDEN
> *President of the SCWT Club of America*

So, the die has been cast. You've made your choice, and a Wheaten puppy will soon be joining your family. If you've done your homework and the puppy has been sourced through proper channels, you may already have a complete list of necessities. Chances are the breeder may have chosen a puppy for you. Don't be surprised if, indeed, this is the case. When properly vetted, breeders know you and your expectations. Consequently, they are often the best judges of which puppy will

Chapter Four: Preparing For Your New Arrival

Photo Courtesy of
Patricia Zurek

> **HELPFUL TIP**
> **Exercise and Prey Drive**
>
> Wheatens are energetic dogs that need plenty of daily exercise. An hour of moderate exercise each day is a good starting place and can include walking, hiking, jogging, or games of fetch. Because Wheatens were initially bred as farm dogs, they often have a high prey drive. As a result, lure coursing may be an excellent option for your Wheaten to blow off steam. While Wheaten terriers are not eligible to compete for AKC titles in lure coursing, this fun activity can be enjoyed by any breed at various locations across the country.

best fit your family and lifestyle. After all, no one knows the personalities and behavioral characteristics of the individual pups in a litter better than their breeder. For example, some Wheaten puppies are naturally more outgoing than others, and if children are part of the equation, a more outgoing puppy is more likely to fill the bill than one that is more retiring. Remember, it is as important to your breeder as it is to you that you and your puppy not only bond well but that you succeed as the new owner of a Wheaten Terrier.

While on the subject of children, it's important that they be readied for the new arrival as well. Make certain that they understand the new rules surrounding the puppy. For example, playtime must be monitored, at least initially, and there are to be well-defined time-outs. Puppies need lots of sleep and rest time, so children need to understand that "crate-time" is quiet time and the puppy is to be left alone. Toys are not to be shared because many kids' toys are unsafe for puppies; the same holds for food.

A Puppy Is not a Stocking Stuffer

A word of caution concerning puppies and children. Giving a puppy as a birthday present or holiday gift is tempting. However, there is no worse time to bring a baby puppy into your home. The level of excitement during a holiday season is quite high, and it is unfair to a puppy to introduce it into your family circle at such a wild and crazy time. If you're determined to purchase a canine as a holiday or birthday gift, one solution is to present

Chapter Four: Preparing For Your New Arrival

gifts that are connected to the puppy, such as the puppy's crate, dog bed, bowls, and a leash. Then, wait until the house has settled down and back into a normal daily routine before introducing a new puppy.

Puppy-proofing Your Home and Yard

> *I consider a securely fenced yard an essential prerequisite for Wheaten ownership. A fence makes housebreaking a much simpler task. With a fenced yard, your kids and Wheaten, or your Wheaten and his dog playmates, can enjoy time outside without the hassle of being tethered. Note: I'm referring to physical fences only. Electric fences have been proven to cause many adverse behavioral issues, including aggression, and can easily leave your dog vulnerable to the danger of escaping from the yard or aggressive wild animals or dogs entering your doge's space. In addition to fencing, it is essential to ensure all plants and landscape materials are dog safe.*
>
> DEBORAH VAN DE VEN
> *Bradberry Soft-Coated Wheaten Terriers*

It is important that you take the same measures you might take when child-proofing your home. Puppies are curious little beings and can get into all sorts of mischief before your very eyes. Before bringing your new Wheaten Terrier home, take some time to do a walk-through of your house, looking for potential dangers. For example, a puppy would love to chew on that electrical cord attached to your table lamp or charger. Electrical outlets, as well, can be curiosities worth your puppy's attention and possibly may be interesting enough to lick. Place electrical cords up and out of reach, at least for the time being. Inexpensive plastic covers for electrical outlets not in use are available at most hardware stores. Keeping doors closed is a good idea. Another solution is to invest in a few "baby gates." Don't forget that many household plants are toxic to animals, among them aloe vera, lilies, ivy, jade, dieffenbachia, caladium, cyclamen, and asparagus fern. So do your homework and either clear your home of those plants that are toxic or make certain they are out of your puppy's reach.

Puppy-proofing the Kitchen

It goes without saying that kitchen cabinets must be kept tightly closed. It is important to remember that dogs, and puppies especially, tend to explore their world with their mouths as well as their noses. Many human foods and most household chemicals are toxic to animals.

Below is a list of some human foods that are toxic to dogs:

- Alcohol, coffee, and caffeine
- Avocado
- Chocolate
- Citrus
- Coconut and coconut oil
- Grapes and raisins
- Nuts, especially macadamia nuts
- Onions, garlic, and chives
- Salt and salty snacks
- Xylitol (used as a sweetener in many products, including gum, candy, baked goods, and toothpaste)
- Yeast dough
- These must be kept well out of your puppy's reach.

Puppy-proofing the Bathroom

Most human medications, along with bathroom chemicals, are toxic to animals and must be kept behind tightly closed cabinets. If you would rather not have toilet paper strewn from one end of your house to the other, keep the bathroom door tightly shut since the temptation is overwhelming for any dog or puppy! Dogs will always be tempted to drink water from the toilet bowl. There are several reasons why this should be prohibited. First, some children forget to flush. Also, some people use toxic cleaning tablets in the tank. Lastly, dogs splash water out of the toilet all over, and no one wants to sit on a wet toilet seat! Rule of thumb—toilet lids should always be kept down.

Chapter Four: Preparing For Your New Arrival

Photo Courtesy of Gay Dunlap

Puppy-proofing the Garage

The dangers inherent in chewing on an electrical cord or cable were mentioned previously and bear repeating in the context of hazards lurking in garages. Other concerns are garbage and trash receptacles, antifreeze (animals like the sweet taste of it), and other toxic chemicals. If your puppy is going to spend time in the garage, make certain that it is a safe place for him.

Puppy-proofing the Garden and Yard

Among the many toxic landscaping plants are azalea, sago palm, foxglove, lily-of-the-valley, daffodils, hydrangeas, holly, and yew. It would be wise to do your own research on exactly what plants in your garden might be toxic and consider either moving or replacing them before bringing home your Wheaten.

Other Potential Hazards

Swimming pools can be the worst hazard of all. Most of us believe that dogs can swim. This, for the most part, is true. However, when a dog falls into a pool, it has no understanding of how to get out. Consequently, it will frantically struggle, clawing at the pool's edge until exhausted, and unless rescued, will sink and drown. Many communities enforce laws that demand pools be fenced. Often, the fencing is for child protection only, and puppies can easily fit through or underneath. You have several choices: one is to add tight mesh wire to the lower perimeter of the fence; another is to teach the puppy where the pool steps are so it can swim its way out. Or you can teach the puppy that the pool is off-limits. Since your puppy will grow into a somewhat heavily coated adult, you probably will not be too enthralled with a Wheaten that loves to leap into the pool for a swim, resulting in a sopping wet Wheaten shaking water all over you and possibly running through the house dripping water everywhere.

Creating a Safe Haven for Your Wheaten

> *A dog's life is to be taken seriously. They are not disposable. Bringing home a pup is comparable to having another child and is a serious time commitment. No matter how badly children want a dog, the responsibility always falls upon the grown-ups. For this reason, bringing in a dog should be a well-thought-out family decision. A high-energy household will often yield a high-energy dog—a failing combination.*
>
> SHARI BOYD
> *ARAN*

All dogs appreciate a safe, comfortable space they can call their own, one to which they can retreat when they need some sleepy time or to get away from the hustle and bustle of family life. Nothing works better

Chapter Four: Preparing For Your New Arrival

Photo Courtesy of Gay Dunlap

than a crate. It keeps your dog safe and out of mischief when you can't be there to supervise and will serve as your primary tool for successful housebreaking. You may want to choose a couple of locations, say, a crate in the family room and another in the bedroom. Setting up a regular schedule for taking the puppy out to potty is the best course of action and will be discussed in detail in Chapter 5.

It is important to consider the age of your children before committing to the addition of a puppy to your family. Very young children are hard-pressed to distinguish between a live puppy and a stuffed animal. The consequences can be grave unless dealt with early on. Not only must you, as the parent, always be in a supervisory mode when small children and the puppy are interacting, but you'll need to be quick to intercede if the interaction leads to conflict or distress on the part of either. Puppies tend to be mouthy, as mentioned earlier, and have sharp little baby teeth. It is an accident waiting to happen when a toddler and a puppy become too immersed in roughhousing. Remember that the puppy can easily deliver a puncture wound, leading to an injured and screaming toddler or the toddler terrorizing the puppy, the latter sometimes leading to an emotionally scarred dog.

Choosing a Veterinarian

> *When choosing a veterinarian, referrals come in handy, as does the familiarity of the doctor with your breed. Prior to bringing your pup home, meet your doctor in person to develop a relationship. A reputable breeder will have suggestions on diet, possibly even on vaccine protocol. Discuss this with your doctor in advance. Advocate for your pet as you would for yourself or loved ones. Discuss options with your breeder. Seek second opinions where warranted.*
>
> SHARI BOYD
> *ARAN*

Choosing a reputable veterinary clinic is a vital aspect of ensuring a lifetime of good health for your Wheaten Terrier. If you live near your puppy's breeder, you can ask the pros and cons of the vet they use, and assuming they offer a positive review, problem solved. If not, the best course of action is to quiz your friends and neighbors with pets. It's a good idea to visit the veterinary facility and ask for a tour. Is it clean? Are there too many people with their pets in the waiting room? Whereas the latter can foretell long wait times, it can also suggest that the clinic is well respected. It also offers an excellent opportunity for off-the-cuff interviews with clients.

From the veterinarian's point of view, a dog is a dog is a dog. In other words, all dog breeds pretty much require the same care and concern medically. This is true, but only up to a point. If the veterinary clinic you have chosen cares for other Soft Coated Wheaten Terriers, they are most likely to be aware of health issues within the breed. Be sure to establish this before your first visit. If not, it would behoove you to provide them with a printout of the health testing requirements laid out on the SCWTCA website (https://scwtca.org/health/health-testing/annual-testing/).

Chapter Four: Preparing For Your New Arrival

You may want to set up a preliminary appointment with a vet to establish that you have a viable line of communication and that the clinic appears to have the best interests of its clients at heart. Sadly, some clinics seem more profit-motivated.

Plan to have the vet see your Wheaten puppy for a complete check-up within the first few days of bringing it home. This means setting up an appointment a few weeks ahead of the puppy's homecoming. Most reputable breeders offer a short-term general health guarantee, and if your Wheaten becomes ill before or shortly after coming to you, you want to be able to document it in order to fall under this guarantee.

Equipment Requirements

In preparation for your puppy's arrival, make certain you are aware of the items required. Some are necessary, while others are suggestions to make you and your puppy a more cohesive unit. All of the items listed will be discussed in more detail under various headings later in this book, e.g., Training, Feeding, Grooming, Exercise.

1. **Crate:** The importance of this item cannot be underscored enough. As mentioned before, a crate is a dog's den. Please do not succumb to calling it a "cage," as this word connotes imprisonment. The crate is for safekeeping and training. It will serve many purposes: potty training, rest time, medical recovery, traveling, cleaning, fires, visitors, vacations, etc. Crates come in various sizes and designs. Some, although rather expensive, serve double duty as pieces of furniture, such as end tables.

2. **Food:** It is best to continue with the brand your breeder recommends, following their schedule and number of feedings per day. Have this food on hand before bringing the puppy home.

3. **Grooming Supplies:** Initially, you will want a comb and brush so that the puppy can get used to grooming early in its life and grow to enjoy it. Your breeder may have suggestions for each grooming implement. If not, a metal comb (Greyhound type) and quality pin

brush should do the trick. If you are planning to clip your puppy's nails, which we highly recommend, invest in a good set of nail clippers and accompanying "Kwik Stop" styptic powder in case you cut the nail a little too close. Slanted tweezers with a scissor handle are handy for removing hair from the inner ear. The latter should be started at about six months and continued throughout your Wheaten's life, every six weeks or so. Puppies always end up needing a bath, usually sooner rather than later. Choose a quality shampoo of the "no tears" variety along with a companion conditioner.

4. **Bedding:** Crate pads are available in sizes that match your crate. It is a good idea to buy two so that you have a change out available. In the early days, and until you have confidence in your Wheaten pup's ability to control its bladder, bedding that is easily thrown into the washer and drier is the best choice.

5. **Bowls:** You need two bowls, one for water and one for food, and they should be sturdy, strong, and not easily tipped over. Water should always be available for your puppy during the daytime hours.

6. **Absorbent Training Pads:** Unless your setup is so convenient that you will be immediately training your puppy to go outside, pee pads are a great interim housebreaking tool. They are also handy for travel. Keep a box or two on hand.

7. **Collar and Lead (Leash):** Rolled leather collars are best suited for the Wheaten Terrier's coat. They treat the neck hair more kindly. Choose a simple cotton web lead with a swivel-style bole snap. Rolled leather collars are usually natural tan, while the leads come in a variety of colors.

8. **Toys and Treats:** It is important that you consider only toys specifically made for dogs. Dog toys will eventually be chewed to pieces, and designers know this. Consequently, there are no parts, such as beady eyes, to be swallowed or choked upon. Some rawhide chew toys are potentially hazardous, as they generally become slimy and can slide down a dog's throat and cause strangulation. Choose your puppy's playthings wisely!

Chapter Four: Preparing For Your New Arrival

9. **Odor Neutralizer and Stain Remover:** No matter how careful you are while housebreaking a puppy (and afterward as well), there will be accidents. If you don't already have both odor neutralizer and stain remover on your laundry shelf, get them before bringing your puppy home.

10. **Poop Bags:** As a responsible dog owner, it is important to be respectful of others. No one is interested in picking up after someone else's dog. Poop bags are designed for ease in picking up after your dog's eliminations. Plan on being a responsible dog owner!

11. **Fencing or Exercise Pen:** Perhaps you already have a fenced-in yard. If not, you may decide to add one or at least fence a small area so that your puppy can exercise free of a leash. Another solution is to purchase an exercise pen. These are also referred to as "puppy playpens." Such pens come in a variety of heights and sizes and are collapsible as well. This also means they are transportable for family vacations, etc.

12. **Dog Gates:** Also called "baby gates," they serve the same general purpose as exercise pens, keeping your puppy either out of specific areas or confined to a specific one. Some dog gates are designed to be permanently installed, while others can be moved as needed.

13. **Dog Car Seat, Harness:** If you plan on traveling with your Wheaten, and most of us do, putting a crate in the back of the car is one solution. It is definitely the safest option. Or you can invest in a dog car seat and/or safety harness. These come with warnings relative to a dog's safety. Remember that most states have stringent laws regarding dogs left in cars in situations wherein their lives are endangered, such as summer heat.

CHAPTER FIVE

Welcoming Your Wheaten Terrier

The big day has finally arrived, and you are picking up your Wheaten Terrier puppy at last. The breeder has asked you to sign a contract detailing her demands and expectations. It no doubt includes an agreement to spay/neuter your puppy at a specified age and to perform yearly health testing through your veterinarian. You have received feeding and basic housebreaking instructions and hopefully a copy of *The Soft Coated Wheaten Terrier Owner's Manual*. Often, breeders will provide a slightly used stuffed toy that has retained all the smells of a puppy's dam and littermates. This will provide the puppy with a degree of comfort as it slowly warms to its new environment. All of that done, the breeder will hand over your puppy.

The Trip Home

You have made all the final preparations at home, gathered the necessary supplies, and made your first appointment with a veterinarian. The last few days have been filled with excitement and anticipation. Whether your Wheaten is close by, a road trip away, or requires an airline flight, there are things you can do to make the trip easier for all concerned.

A crate is doubtless the safest mode of transportation for your Wheaten; one primary reason is that when accidents occur, dogs riding loose in a car are usually thrown out of the vehicle since there is nothing to stop their momentum. Some breeders introduce their pups to a crate early on, a bonus since the puppy has already grown accustomed to it. Hopefully, this will be the case for you. A small crate is best, transitioning

Chapter Five: Welcoming Your Wheaten Terrier

Photo Courtesy of Gay Dunlap

to a larger one as the puppy grows closer to its adult size. Line the crate with plenty of paper toweling or shredded newsprint (also called packing paper). The latter shreds into narrow strips quite easily, and any eliminations are quickly lost in it. Your breeder will probably have had the foresight to skip the meal closest to your pick-up time. You might want to request this just to be on the safe side. Trust that no puppy ever died for lack of a meal or two!

If you are depending upon an airline, there was a time when shipping puppies via air cargo was the norm. However, times have changed with canceled and delayed flights, staffing problems, and other airline complications. Most breeders will suggest you fly out to pick the puppy up, returning home with it in a carry-on bag that fits under the seat. Such bags, the Sherpa, for example, are soft-sided and airline-compliant. Often, breeders will loan you a bag with an understanding that it will be returned. If flying is your preferred mode of pick-up, make certain your breeder provides you with the paperwork required by the airlines, typically a valid, up-to-date health certificate and record of inoculations signed by a licensed veterinarian.

Unless your breeder lives around the corner, the drive home with your puppy involves a bit of planning, too. Depending upon the length of the trip, you should carry sufficient water, along with a small bowl, as well as a collar and leash, so that the puppy can relieve itself along the way. Plan on potty breaks for road trips of over an hour; young puppies may need breaks as often as every couple of hours. Only offer water at these times, allowing at least 20 minutes afterward for the puppy to relieve itself before starting off again. Bring along paper towels for clean-up and in case the puppy gets carsick. A couple of pee pads for the rest stops and waste disposal baggies should round out your "Be Prepared" list. If you are driving alone, plan on putting the puppy in a crate (as described above), with the possible addition of a toy or two. If the family is coming too, then the puppy will no doubt be held in a loving lap, although it should be remembered that a crate is always the safest place!

The First Night

> **"**
>
> *I recommend placing the crate beside your bed for the first week or two. Since the puppy likely hasn't slept all alone yet, and he's in a new environment, having the puppy sleep in a crate in your room (not on your bed) helps you bond, and will hopefully allow you to get some sleep. You can also hear if he needs to relieve himself.*
>
> SHARI ROBINSON
> *Keepsake Wheatens*
>
> **"**

The first night is always the hardest. Everyone is most likely quite excited. Encourage children to be gentle and calm. If you have other pets, it's best to wait a while before introducing them to the newcomer. The same goes for introducing neighbors and friends. Plan on giving the puppy ample time to become familiar with the new surroundings and immediate family before adding other stimuli. "Keep it simple" is a good

Chapter Five: Welcoming Your Wheaten Terrier

motto for the first few days. You might consider two small crates initially, one for the kitchen and one for the bedroom. Remember, this is the puppy's own space, its bed, its sanctuary, and the sooner that's established, the better. Feeding in the kennel is an excellent idea since it reinforces the notion not only that it is the puppy's space but also that it is not a place to be soiled. Water must be made available at all hours during the day but should be removed overnight. There are food bowls and water dispensers on the market, some specifically designed for crate use. These help keep messy eating and water sloshing to a minimum.

The puppy should sleep in his kennel (the crate) beginning with the very first night. Chances are that the puppy will cry, especially if the breeder has not accustomed him to a crate. Please do not weaken. Stand your ground. If you let your puppy out whenever he cries, the message becomes loud and clear, and your puppy will quickly learn that screaming at three in the morning gets rewarded. This is a job that takes self-discipline, to be sure. You and your family may experience a few sleepless nights, but in the end, your diligence will win out with the puppy giving in and settling down. There is a product on the market that may help settle him—a small stuffed animal that creates warmth and mimics a beating heart.

Whatever you do, keep the faith! Your perseverance will pay off sooner rather than later if you are consistent. Still, do not automatically assume that your Wheaten puppy will go through the night without a potty break. Some will and some won't. If he has been sleeping quietly for several hours and suddenly awakens, pick the puppy up and take him outside. Picking him up and carrying him out is crucial. If you don't, in all probability, he will immediately squat and pee on your favorite rug. Trust me! As soon as he has finished with his business, pick him up and carry him back inside to bed. The middle of the night or a ridiculously early morning hour is not the time for play. He may cry a little again before dropping off to sleep. Remember, dogs thrive on consistency. If you are firm and consistent during these early training months, the unwanted puppy behaviors will soon disappear. Develop a planned routine with the puppy and stick to it. If you find you must make a few adjustments, feel free to do so, but remember to be consistent with the new routine.

And The Next Morning

> **"**
>
> *I always suggest that people have a crate ready for their new puppy and ideally a safe area set aside that is just for the puppy. This is where he should be placed when he is not being actively watched by you so that accidents don't happen, such as urinating on the floor or chewing on shoes.*
>
> DENISE BENDELEWSKI
> *Dhowden Soft Coated Wheaten Terriers*
> **"**

Thus begins life with your Wheaten Terrier pup. There is nothing like the present to begin laying down the rules of life for your new dog. Set a daily schedule, beginning now. The puppy is taken out first thing in the morning to do his business. Verbal praising is in order when the puppy does what he should—good puppy! Then, into the kitchen, where breakfast is presented, preferably in the kennel. The puppy will probably be ravenous—good puppy again when he finishes his food—then

Chapter Five: Welcoming Your Wheaten Terrier

it's up and outside. If the puppy pees or poops, another praise, and back in the house for a little free romp before being placed back in the kennel.

The idea here is to set up a routine such that your Wheaten puppy accustoms himself to his "space," understanding that it is his alone and that he is expected to do his business outside before being allowed the freedom to romp around the house. Doubtless, there will be accidents, but with this rou-

HELPFUL TIP
Which Color Will I Be?

Most Wheaten terriers are born with dark brown coats, but how can you tell which color they'll be when they grow up? Wheaten Terriers' coats lighten as they age and usually become pale beige or golden in adulthood. According to the SCWTCA breed standard, an occasional black or red guard hair is permitted, but the entirety of the coat should be wheaten, although blue-grey coloring is common on the ears and muzzle.

tine, there will be far fewer. The same procedure should be followed all day, with lunch and dinner handled in the same manner, although by the time you pick the puppy up, the breeder may have reduced his meals to two a day instead of three. In no time at all, your Wheaten pup will get the picture, and you will reward him with more and more romp time. It is then that you will find him retreating to his kennel of his own volition, ready for a nap or some alone time with his toys.

If you have another pet or pets, you might want to wait for a day before slowly introducing them to their new "brother" or "sister." You want to be careful that the old guard does not overwhelm or intimidate your Wheaten puppy or, conversely, that the bouncy youngster does not threaten your old-timer. Introducing animals in a large space, such as the family room or perhaps the yard, is wise since meeting in close quarters, such as the hallway, could be perceived by one animal or the other as a hostile environment with no escape.

It is not unusual for a pecking order to be established among your family of pets. Be forewarned, however, that two might vie for alpha position, especially if the puppy was dominant in his litter. It is a clash that must be put to rest in order to establish a peaceful kingdom. Be patient and allow the dogs time away from each other, especially if your older dog is geriatric since a puppy can be stressful. This break from the puppy will be much appreciated. You might want to rotate exercise time out, one dog in its crate while the other is out.

Cats are another matter, and, generally speaking, the best policy is for your cat to befriend your Wheaten on its own terms. Never force an interaction between them. Do not allow either of them to chase or pounce upon the other. Rather, redirect the puppy to a toy or a game of tug-a-war and reward him with a treat for leaving the cat alone. If your cat is the aggressor, the best solution is still to redirect the puppy! All good things come in time and with patience!

Shari Boyd with one of her Wheatens

Chapter Five: Welcoming Your Wheaten Terrier

First Visit to the Vet

You have no doubt chosen a veterinarian, made an appointment, and the time has come for your first visit, which should be within the first week of the puppy's arrival. It's a good idea to jot down any questions you might have beforehand since we all tend to forget important concerns in the distractions of the moment. The ability to address your concerns and ask your questions succinctly will be appreciated by your vet since it speaks to your respect for his time and expertise.

You want to make this first trip to the vet as enjoyable as possible. If you have a young puppy, you might want to bring a few treats with you. Since there will be other animals in the waiting room, you will want to keep your Wheaten close to you on a tight leash. Remember that not all dogs are thrilled with being at the vet, so this is not a good time for socializing with them. When you check in, mention that you have your Wheaten's health and birth records, along with DNA test results, from the breeder with you. The receptionist may want to copy them for your pup's file.

You will probably be asked to weigh your puppy before being ushered into an exam room. Here, you will be asked a few questions about the dog's current health, any medications being given, and what you are feeding. After a short wait, the veterinarian will enter, examine your Wheaten from end to end, and probably take the puppy's temperature. If there are any vaccines due, they will be administered as well. Now is the time to ask any questions.

This is also a good time to decide if you want to consider pet insurance. Most pet insurance plans exclude pre-existing conditions. They also require waiting periods. Consequently, if you are going to do it, the best time to sign up is sooner rather than later. Pet insurance will be discussed in detail in Chapter 10.

CHAPTER SIX

Training

The job of training a puppy can be considered in one of two ways. It can be looked upon as an unpleasant but necessary chore, or it can be channeled into a rewarding and delightful hobby for the owner. Taking on retraining a rescue dog is quite another matter. In truth, many rescue dogs are in shelters as the result of owners giving up on dogs they failed to properly train. Housebreaking heads the list of failures. Although housebreaking may be hard to envision as a hobby, its importance is obvious. No one wants a dog that piddles and poops whenever and wherever it chooses.

Housebreaking

The goal here is to instill good habits and build a loving bond between you and your puppy. The recipe for success requires consistency, patience, and positive reinforcement. By positive reinforcement, we mean praising your Wheaten puppy when he holds his bladder and bowels, eliminating outside in a designated place. Scolding the puppy for soiling his kennel or squatting on the living room rug serves only to confuse the puppy and does nothing to foster the loving bond you are hoping to build. The method that works best is to confine the puppy to a well-defined space. It might be a small room or simply keeping the puppy on a relatively tight leash that is attached to you. However, as suggested earlier in this book, the best method of confinement is a crate.

Keep the puppy on a regular feeding schedule, feed him in his crate, and take the food bowl away between meals. Water must always be available to him during the day but should be removed during the nighttime hours. Carry the puppy out first thing in the morning, after each meal,

Chapter Six: Training

and whenever he awakens from a nap. Typically, the schedule should dictate that your puppy is taken out every 30 minutes to an hour. In other words, in the early stages of housebreaking, you are "beating him to the draw." This procedure also allows you the best possible opportunity for positive reinforcement. It helps if you take the puppy to the same spot each time since the scent left there previously will prompt him to go.

Allow the puppy romp time in the house immediately following the successful evacuation of his bladder and bowels when you are more confident that it will not have an accident. Then, put him back in his crate. If this amount of crate time seems harsh, remember that your consistency and persistence will ensure that the training period is a short one, and in no time at all, your puppy will be housebroken and trustworthy. Then, the crate will only be used at night, when the puppy is home alone, and during times when he cannot be supervised.

You may want to consider installing a doggy door, especially if you are away a lot during the day. Make sure the door size will accommodate a mature Wheaten Terrier. It's important to establish that the outside area on the other side of the door is completely safe. Ideally, it should be walled or fenced off and completely inaccessible to other animals. It should also be gated and/or locked so that other people have no access to your dog. Training your Wheaten to use the doggy door requires two people, one on the inside and the other outside. Start with the flap off the door. The outside person will call the puppy while the inside person helps by pushing him through the opening. Then, the outside person will reward your Wheaten when he gets there, either verbally or with a treat. Repeat this until the puppy gets the picture and goes in and out successfully on his own. Then, add the flap and repeat the process several times until he gets it. You may have to lift the corner of the flap initially. Slowly lift less and less of the flap until the dog pushes through from both sides without your help.

As much as we love our dogs and wish to take them with us wherever we go, this is often not possible. As stated earlier, the safest place for a dog when you are not at home is in his crate, with sufficient water and a few toys. This is especially true with puppies. Untold mischief can be the result of a puppy left unsupervised at home. I once had a puppy rummage through a guest's open suitcase, whereupon she discovered a small plastic pill bag. The puppy was able to chew it open and swallow one of the pills. It could have ended in tragedy. Fortunately, it did not. Consider if there was a fire in your home while you were away. Imagine a dog, whether puppy or adult, running in fear from the firemen trying to save it, as opposed to being ensconced in a crate, easily picked up and carried to safety.

FAMOUS WHEATENS
Diving Dog

A seven-year-old Wheaten Terrier named Krista made history in 2016 when she jumped 10 feet and 2 inches at the national dock diving championship in Orlando, Florida. Though Krista fell just short of placing in the top 10 dogs at the tournament, she was the first Wheaten Terrier to compete in the diving event. In the preliminary events, Krista took home a first-place ribbon and two third-place awards.

Chapter Six: Training

Basic Commands

> *It is important to remember that despite your puppy being like a baby, it isn't a human baby! This is a dog, with dog instincts, and it's important not to let him believe he's in charge of decisions. My favorite term is 'we don't negotiate with Terriers.' Dogs, like young children, don't actually live in a democracy. They need training, guidance, and boundaries. To have a well-balanced adult dog, you want that training consistent when he's young.*
>
> SHARI ROBINSON
> *Keepsake Wheatens*

Many training issues are born out of owners allowing their pups to get away with unacceptable behavior because they find it cute or funny. Then, as the puppy matures, the humor is gone, and the behavior becomes irritating, exasperating, or worse. Some behaviors left unchecked can be a life-or-death matter for your Wheaten. For example, an untrained, undisciplined dog that bounds out through an open door or backyard gate with no knowledge of "sit," "come," or "stay" may soon be a dead dog. Working with your puppy on obedience training is not just about teaching good manners. It also serves as a channel for bonding and building a strong relationship between you and your Wheaten. Although the focus here is on training a puppy, these methods are certainly applicable to an older dog as well. It's always easier, however, to start with a blank slate.

Dogs, in general, are not deliberately naughty, nor do they intend to displease us. They are simply being dogs. They want to please us but need clarity and comprehension. At the same time, it is difficult for a dog to learn in an atmosphere where it is constantly in fear of punishment. Wheaten Terriers, more than most, can become particularly fearful and confused when faced with situations they don't understand. They do not function well in a punitive environment. Training methods that involve even a hint of negative verbal reprimand or physical abuse will turn your

Wheaten into a lackluster, unwilling worker instead of a happy, enthusiastic one. Such methods easily become a source of stress and even fear.

Basic commands, starting with your puppy responding to his name, should begin early. As early as seven weeks, a puppy is capable of learning to "sit," "come," and "stay." Short sessions of no more than 15 or 20 minutes a day should fit easily into your schedule. That's also all the training a puppy's attention span can handle. It's vitally important, however, to hold to a daily training routine since puppies will easily forget what was taught the day before. Ask any athlete about the importance of repetition in training muscles. It's the same with all training. Repetition, repetition, repetition! One owner, whose 10-week-old puppy had begun to sound off with a rather loud bark, taught him within a few days of repetition and treats to do "silent bark!" All things are possible with patience, repetition, and enthusiasm!

Sit

Of the three basic commands, "Sit" must come first. It is the foundation for the other two commands and lays the groundwork for any other obedience work you may choose to do with your Wheaten. It is also a command that will be useful in keeping your dog safe and for curbing his impulses. You will want to find a quiet place to work with your puppy. Start by holding a treat in your hand and move it in front of your puppy's mouth and nose until you get his attention. Let him sniff and maybe take a nibble. Move the treat above his head and say, "Sit." Slowly move the treat up about three inches over his head and slightly behind it. Say "sit" again. Since you are moving the treat, the puppy will look at it, which causes him to look up and naturally sit. The minute his butt hits the ground, say, "Good sit!" and give him the treat. If this doesn't work, move a step closer to the puppy so that he must look up even higher. This tends to lead into a natural sitting position. As soon as his bottom hits the floor,

Chapter Six: Training

enthusiastically and happily say, "Good sit!" and reward him with the treat. Repeated use of the word "sit" further cements in the dog's mind the action that just occurred.

About 10–15 repetitions should be done each session in a calm, comfortable area where your puppy is free to focus without distractions. It's a good idea to count out your treats beforehand so you can keep track of your repetitions.

Stay

Once your puppy has mastered the "sit," begin to work on "stay" by encouraging the dog to remain sitting for a few seconds before rewarding him. Rewarding can be the usual training treat, an enthusiastic response, a pat, a rub, or whatever makes your puppy the happiest. Trying other methods of reward is a good idea since you do not want your dog to require bribing for everything. Ask him to sit again, but wait a few seconds longer this time before rewarding him. Continue along this vein, gradually adding more and more seconds until the puppy is sitting for at least 15 seconds.

Continue until you feel secure that your puppy can be trusted to hold the sit for this length of time. Then, begin to use the word "stay." Simply say "sit," wait for the puppy to sit, then say "stay," not forgetting to treat or reward for his obedience! It is recommended that you spend 15–30 minutes each day on this exercise until you can totally rely upon your pup's holding the stay command. This can be a bit difficult, especially if your puppy is easily distracted. But don't give up. If you find yourself getting frustrated or impatient, step back and give it a break. Come back tomorrow with the faith that your puppy will eventually get it. When he does, it's time to teach the release command.

Release from Stay

Ask your puppy to sit. Then wait 15 seconds before throwing a treat toward him in such a way that the puppy must get up to retrieve it at the very same time as you give the release signal, which might be a simple raising of your hand or a verbal command such as "go" or "okay."

Your pup's full comprehension of the "stay" command opens the door to more challenging exercises, such as increasing the distance between you and your puppy or having him hold the stay for longer periods of time. You can also practice the exercise while on walks or in diverse environments. Remember, however, that the stay command is designed for relatively short periods of time to keep your dog safe. Never use the stay command for extended periods of time or in perilous situations.

Come

This is the last of the "Basic Commands." As with the others, you must start in a safe, quiet place with no distractions. This might be your fenced-in yard or in the house. Begin when your puppy is not close to you by calling his name and saying the word "come." Always use the same word and never diverge from it. You can begin to praise the puppy even if he simply turns to look at you. Keep the praise coming until he gets there. As soon as he reaches you, give him treat after treat after treat, at the same time showering him with so much verbal praise that he thinks he's won the lottery! You might also want to give him scratches, pets, and rubs.

Remember to keep your tone fun and your voice happy. If you sound tough, stern, or angry, the puppy's instinct will be to avoid you. Never ever call your puppy to scold him. Let him go back to exploring for a bit, then repeat the "come" command and provide the same sorts of rewards when he gets to you. You might also surprise him with his favorite toy. Spend 15–20 minutes each day training until your

Chapter Six: Training

puppy is convinced that coming to you when you call him is the happiest moment of his life!

The same basic rules apply when teaching these basic commands to an older dog. It may not be quite so easy since older dogs can be more set in their ways, but on the other hand, they are not so easily distracted. Just remember, never ask your dog to come if you are planning to scold him or follow it up with something you know he dislikes, such as a bath or a nail trimming. Don't start a training session if you are upset, feeling rushed, or in a bad mood. Only ask him to come when your intention is to heap praise upon him. Then, he will trust you and become confident that only good things happen when you call him.

If you don't have a safe and secure area, there is another method that requires the use of a 30'–50' lead (also called a leash). Attach the lead to your dog's collar, the lead coiled up in your hand. Give the "stay" command and slowly back away, uncoiling the lead as you go. The first few times, keep the distance between you and the dog short until he gets the idea, call him to you, and reward him when he comes (with both treats and praise). Continue in this manner, letting more and more of the lead out until you reach the end of it and your dog comes to you. Work with him in this manner, with you at the end of the lead, for several days until he comes to you every time. Then you are probably ready to try working with him off-lead.

Walking on Lead

Be forewarned that Wheaten Terriers are notorious for pulling on a lead; a pulling, gagging, and choking dog ruins the otherwise pleasant walking experience. So does dragging an unwilling puppy. As with all training exercises, begin with patience. Do not put a leash on your puppy unless you have a lot of time and nowhere special to go. Your objective must be simply to make the next 15 minutes or so a joyful time. Put a collar on your puppy, preferably rolled leather, not too tight but not so loose that he might wriggle out of it, and put some treats in your pocket. Attach a leash and step away from him. If he bounds along with you,

great. If he doesn't, call him with a happy voice and immediately reward him if he comes.

If your puppy is refusing to walk with you, it's because this is new to him, and he is scared. Just keep up with a cheery manner until he feels more secure. Start to walk with him at your side, left side preferable, encouraging him to continue on with treats and praise. Once the puppy decides this walking business is fun, he may start to pull ahead of you or decide to pull one way or another. If he does, just stop! He will probably turn around to look at you. Gently tug him back into position next to you, or pick him up and put him back down at your side with praise and a treat. If he starts to pull again, stop and begin to back up. Once again, he will probably turn to look at you.

Remember, dogs like consistency, and if you let the puppy get away with pulling once, he'll try it again! Repeat the process, putting him back in position beside you. When it's appropriate, and you're in a safe place, stop and allow him some exploring and sniffing time, but *never* let him pull you. Leash manners take a bit more time and persistence than other training exercises, but they are vitally important both for you and your dog. Constant pulling, when it is obviously against your wishes, puts your dog in charge, at least in his mind. It can also cause serious cervical problems for the dog down the road.

Physical and Mental Exercises

Learning basic commands might be considered equivalent to your puppy graduating from kindergarten. It sets the stage for more advanced activity, both physical and mental. You now know that your Wheaten Terrier is capable of learning activities that will expand his physical and mental competency in the dog world! Of course, they include the old standbys like obedience and agility, but there is also so much more. There

Chapter Six: Training

Photo Courtesy of Susana Figueiredo

are field trials and myriad performance sports. Some of those available are barn hunt, designed especially for terriers, herding, scent work, dock diving, fly ball, lure coursing, and fast cat. There are many others. Involve yourself in any of these, and you just might turn your dog's vitality and excitement into a gratifying hobby for yourself.

Some Wheaten Terriers are happy being couch potatoes. Others love the sense that they are "contributing" to their home and hearth. Your Wheaten might enjoy being of service by bringing you your slippers or perhaps the morning paper. Job or not, if you sense your Wheaten is trying to tell you something, don't ignore him. It might be something so simple as the desire to snuggle up with you while you watch TV. It might also be, "I need to go potty!" Pay attention.

> *Wheatens love to be involved. If you don't provide positive play, they will create their own. Play original games or explore the internet for ideas.*
>
> **EMILY HOLDEN**
> *President of the SCWT Club of America*

The Importance of Early Socialization

> *The importance of socialization cannot be stressed enough. From the importance of preparing your pup for a lifetime of grooming to planning holiday trips to visit family and interact with other family members' pets or children ... The list goes on and must be considered before bringing your pup home, so as to carefully develop your course of action. A daily and continuing plan must be implemented. To incorporate a pup into your home, not socialize said pup to children, and then, three years later, start your family, is potentially a human failure.*
>
> **SHARI BOYD**
> *ARAN*

Chapter Six: Training

Socializing your puppy is more far-reaching than simply introducing him to other dogs in the neighborhood. It's about introducing him to the entire big, wide world out there. It is crucial that socialization be foremost in your training plans. The goal is to instill in your dog the understanding that there is absolutely nothing anywhere to fear. If your puppy was purchased from a responsible hobby breeder, socialization has already begun since the optimum age for processing new experiences is quite early, starting at three weeks.

One mistake new owners make is to be overprotective until their puppy has had his series of inoculations. Do not make the mistake of thinking your puppy must be protected from others until he has had all his shots. Dogs do not need all three shots to ensure total immunization. The reason for the repetition is that there is no way of determining when the natural immunization he received from his dam has worn off. Hence, the three-shot regimen over a period of three months assumes one of them will take up the slack, leaving the puppy successfully immunized.

The American Veterinary Society of Animal Behavior believes that it should be standard practice for puppies to receive socialization before they are fully vaccinated. Members point out that behavioral problems are the greatest threat to the owner-dog bond, and, in fact, they are the number one cause of relinquishment to shelters. Behavioral issues, not infectious diseases, are the number one cause of death for dogs under three years of age. There are several avenues available for helping you with the socialization of your Wheaten Terrier, whether puppy or adult. They will be discussed in detail in Chapter 8.

Photo Courtesy of Jill Moran

CHAPTER SEVEN

Grooming

> *You may plan to use a professional groomer for your Wheaten, so you're wondering why you need a grooming table. For a couple of reasons, actually. First, your puppy needs to learn to accept standing on the grooming table without struggling, stressing, or nipping. Short sessions at home, with him standing calmly, will teach him that grooming is a pleasant experience instead of something to be feared. Secondly, your puppy will need at least weekly brushing, combing, and toenail trimming his entire life. A Wheaten who only receives grooming once every six weeks at a grooming shop is destined to be unkempt, with matted hair, and will be a difficult, poorly behaved client. Set your puppy up for success by starting his grooming routine early.*
>
> DEBORAH VAN DE VEN
> *Bradberry Soft-Coated Wheaten Terriers*

If you are considering the addition of a Soft Coated Wheaten Terrier to your family, there should be little doubt in your mind that a commitment to hair care is a prerequisite. If this isn't made clear, then the breeder has failed. The Wheaten Terrier is a breed whose coat requires a great deal of attention. In addition to being part of its name, the Wheaten Terrier's coat is, at maturity, its crowning glory. Ideally, the texture is soft and silky, lying flat against the body with a gentle wave. The color is described as any "any shade of wheat," which may range from off-white to a deep golden hue.

Chapter Seven: Grooming

Photo Courtesy of Gay Dunlap

In the canine world, there are two basic types of coats. One is generally referred to as "fur" and the other as "hair." Dogs with "fur" have a double coat, wherein a soft undercoat lies beneath a protective hard outercoat. These are the coats that shed. Dogs with "hair" may or may not have an undercoat. Those that are single-coated either shed very little or not at all. While no breed is truly hypoallergenic, breeds with single coats are less apt to disperse allergens into the air since they do not shed. But because hair is finer than fur, it tends to trap particles and dead follicles more easily. It also attracts various sorts of debris, which in turn cause mats and knots to form. The Wheaten Terrier has hair, is single-coated, and does not shed. Although it is a blessing in so many ways, this type of coat offers up a different set of problems, as it will quite readily tangle, knot, and mat.

Don't be surprised if your Wheaten puppy's coat appears quite different from that of his mother or any other adult Wheaten Terrier you may have run into. It may even appear to be a double coat. This fluffy puppy coat will slowly give way to the flat, lustrous, wavy coat of the mature Wheaten Terrier somewhere around a year of age. Meanwhile, it is imperative that you start brushing and combing your puppy's coat immediately. It isn't a matter of whether the coat needs it, but rather that he understands it is an activity to which he must become accustomed, hopefully to the point where he begins to enjoy it. Your manner of handling this will be the determining factor. If your grooming approach is gentle and soothing, your puppy will be happy to oblige. Otherwise, you will soon find that there is nothing more exasperating than trying to brush and comb a dog that is fighting you tooth and nail. The outcome of this often is an owner that gives up, resorting to a professional groomer and a grooming salon that may refuse to accept the dog as a client, or worse. By worse, I mean a frustrated, irritated groomer who hurts or otherwise mistreats the dog.

Please understand that the Wheaten Terrier requires thorough brushing and combing daily or, at the very least, every other day, regardless of whether you choose to use a professional grooming service or not. It is an activity that should be part of your daily routine. Keeping this commitment ensures that your Wheaten's coat and skin both remain healthy and beautiful. If you are unable to meet this obligation, you should consider another breed.

The grooming process can be done initially by simply sitting on the floor in front of the TV, putting your puppy on one side and then the other, gently brushing through his coat from stem to stern, including the legs, with either a pin or slicker brush and following up with a comb. Early on, your puppy must begin learning to tolerate not only gentle brushing and combing but nail clipping and the gentle handling of his ears, mouth, and paws. It is important that these early grooming sessions be kept short and fun. More on this later in the chapter.

Chapter Seven: Grooming

Why a Grooming Table?

Sooner or later, you will find the purchase of a grooming table and arm to be a wise investment. In many ways, it makes sense to begin your grooming procedure by accustoming your puppy to being placed on the table for all aspects of physical care. An accompanying grooming arm with attached noose helps to keep the puppy in a stable position. Remember, however, to never leave your Wheaten unattended on the table, especially with his neck in a grooming noose. It sets the stage for certain tragedy.

As with all training practices, it is important that the puppy finds grooming, if not a joyful experience, at least a pleasant one. In the beginning, in addition to keeping these sessions short, praise and treats should abound, especially for the handling of paws and examining the mouth. For example, every time you lift a paw or ear flap, follow it with praise! You also want the puppy accustomed to having his teeth brushed.

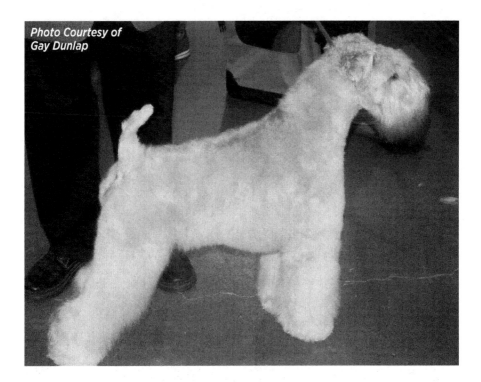

Photo Courtesy of Gay Dunlap

HISTORICAL FACT
Tail Docking

Soft Coated Wheaten Terriers have historically had their tails docked a few days after birth. This was true for most Terriers throughout the British Isles and Ireland was no exception. This practice most likely began as an effort to avoid paying taxes. In the 18th century, only landowners and members of the aristocracy were allowed dogs, kept, primarily for hunting/sport. They certainly did not want the tenant farmer encroaching on their sport. A high tax was levied on the owners of such dogs and one way to avoid paying them was to dock a dog's tail. There was another reason though. It was thought that the practice of tail docking helped to ward off rabies. Although docked tails are still part of the Wheaten's breed standard in this country, undocked tails are also permitted. In recent years, many countries throughout the world have outlawed tail docking.

Although puppy teeth do not require it, you should prepare him for a time in the future when his teeth will definitely require attention.

Your ultimate goal is to have a Wheaten Terrier that loves his time on the grooming table because he knows he will be the center of your attention and rewarded for good behavior! Making grooming a regular part of his life, with regular brushing and combing, ensures that there is no chance for the accumulation of matted hair or knots, both of which will undoubtedly create pain when they have to be forcibly removed.

Regardless of how you begin these early grooming sessions, on the floor or on a table, they should be kept short and with lots of praise. Say, "Good puppy!" every time you briefly lift a paw or ear flap and every time you take a quick peek inside the mouth.

Grooming Tools

Make certain you have all the necessary grooming tools. As mentioned earlier, you will want a good quality brush, either a pin brush or slicker brush and a quality steel comb with a combination of fine/coarse tines and sharp teeth (preferably the ones referred to as Greyhound or Greyhound-type). Some combs have blunt teeth and are useless on a

Chapter Seven: Grooming

Photo Courtesy of Gay Dunlap

Wheaten coat. You should also have nail clippers and styptic powder, blunt-nosed tweezers or hemostats, a pair of blunt-nosed scissors, a toothbrush and doggy toothpaste, and a quality tearless dog shampoo and conditioner.

Grooming the Wheaten Terrier

Assuming your Wheaten has become acclimated to the grooming table, begin by back-brushing his leg furnishings from the skin out. This means against the downward growth of hair (layering from foot up to elbow) on all sides of each leg. Continue in the same manner with the body coat, one side at a time, lifting the coat in layers (line brushing), beginning at the underbelly and brushing one layer at a time until the back is reached, including the tail, and you are confident no mats or tangles have been left.

Move around to face your dog from the front and line brush his beard and fall, lifting up the hair in layers and brushing down, following up with the fine teeth of your comb to make sure there are no mats, especially close to the mouth. Then, begin to comb the body coat down using the same layering technique, making certain the comb does not get caught up in any snags or mats that may have been missed, and finish up by combing the hair on the dog's head (the fall) and his beard. Pay particular attention to the areas between the chest and elbow, the underbelly, around the genitals, and the beard, where mats are more apt to form.

Although nutrition will be discussed at length in Chapter 10, it should be mentioned here that a healthy, nutritionally balanced diet plays a major role in the health of a dog's skin and coat.

Bath Time

Regular bathing every couple of weeks or so also helps to maintain the health of your Wheaten's coat and skin. Bathing, in addition to making your dog more "huggable," keeps matting well under control since

Chapter Seven: Grooming

a clean coat, other than looking beautiful, is free of debris and less apt to clumping.

One important rule to remember: NEVER BATHE A MATTED DOG. In other words, always go through the brushing and combing routine before bathing. Not doing so will triple the amount of work required to remove tangles and mats.

Early on, the kitchen or laundry room sink is quite suitable for bathing your puppy. If the faucet does not include a showerhead, it can easily be attached to the existing one. A small rubber mat will keep the puppy from slipping. Have plenty of towels on hand before you start, and be sure to test the water temperature before wetting the puppy down. Remember that dogs have a higher body temperature than we do, so slightly warmer water will feel more comfortable on their skin. Here again, comforting words and jubilant praise will set the stage for a pleasant experience.

Wet the puppy down thoroughly before applying a good-quality tear-less dog shampoo, working it up into a rich lather, and saving the head for last. Be careful not to get water in the ear canal. If you are concerned about this, you can always stuff small cotton balls into the dog's ears. Just remember to remove them when bathing is done. Fully rinse out all shampoo before applying the conditioner (also tearless) and, again, rinse, rinse, rinse thoroughly. Even the slightest trace of shampoo left in the coat will be readily removed with the use of conditioner, which is why it is an important step in the bathing process. Do not allow yourself to be talked into a "leave-in" conditioner. Such products actually attract dirt.

For an adult Wheaten, follow the same procedure as described above, using your bathtub and a flexible hose with an attached showerhead. Be sure the dog has secure footing, and if the tub does not have a nonslip surface, put a rubber bath mat on the bathtub floor.

Once bathing is complete, squeeze excess water out of the coat and allow your dog lots of shaking before drying him further with towels. Depending upon your climate and/or the time of year, he may be allowed to dry naturally in the summer months or when the weather is sufficiently warm.

A suitable alternative is the use of a hairdryer. This is when your grooming table comes into play once again. For young puppies, you might want to place a thick towel over your legs and dry the dog in your lap. Otherwise, spread a dry towel out on the table and stand the dog there with his head in the noose. With the hairdryer set on warm, begin to blow and back brush his coat, one section at a time, from the hindquarters to the chest and front legs, making certain one area is completely dry before moving on to another. Set the dryer to low before moving on to your Wheaten's face. It is a good idea to leave the head for last as this allows it to partially dry on its own and gives your dog time to adjust to the hairdryer before hitting him in the face with it. Once completely dry, comb through the coat so that it lies flat, and you are now gazing upon your beautiful Wheaten Terrier in all his glory!

Nails, Ears, and Teeth, etc.

Other grooming tasks include keeping the nails short, teeth clean, and the ears both clean and dry. Terrier nails tend to grow faster than other breeds, especially in puppies. It is recommended that the nails be cut back every week or two in their early stages. As noted earlier, it's important to get your Wheaten puppy used to having his paws handled. With your puppy, begin by speaking softly as you massage each paw, gently separating the toes. He may instinctively pull away. If this happens, repeat whatever it was he didn't like, but do it more slowly and gently until he begins to accept it. When you think he's ready, cut one or two nails and have a treat ready for positive reinforcement. With patience, you can also train an older dog in the same manner.

Cutting an adult Wheaten's nails once a month or so is adequate. Nails are quite soft following a bath, so this is an ideal time to do it. Cut the nails back to the quick evenly, using whatever type of clipper you prefer, and always keep styptic powder close by in case you draw blood. It's important to keep your dog's nails short. Not only can long nails cause your Wheaten pain and discomfort, but they can be hazardous to others, including children. If you find you can't trim them yourself, ask your vet or a professional groomer to handle it for you. Another tool for shortening a dog's nails is a battery-operated Dremel. Using the sander/grinder attachment, small amounts are taken off gradually with no concerns about hitting the quick. Dogs seem better

Chapter Seven: Grooming

able to handle this method. When using a Dremel, push the hair back from the nail so that none is caught in it.

Regularly check your Wheaten's ears by lifting the earflap. Bath time, of course, is the perfect time to do this. Make certain the underside of the earflap is clean and that no unpleasant odor is emanating from the ear canal. With your blunt-nosed tweezers or hemostats, remove any hair inside the canal. This often occurs in the ears of single-coated dogs and, if allowed to accumulate, can cause chronic ear infections. Using a cotton pad moistened with warm water to swab out the ear is a good idea as well.

Your puppy's baby teeth will have been replaced with permanent ones by the time he is around six or seven months old. Keeping these adult teeth clean is crucial to his health. Not only will periodontal disease cause your Wheaten extreme discomfort and putrid breath, but it can also predispose him to life-threatening disease. To prepare him for dental care such as regular teeth brushing, it's wise to accustom your puppy to having his mouth opened and examined. Remember, it's a training process, so make it lighthearted, and don't be afraid to be silly, even making it into a game! Once your dog's permanent teeth are in, plan on brushing them every other day or so, using canine toothpaste and a doggy toothbrush. Some doggy toothbrushes slip over your finger to make brushing easier. Lifting the lip of a Wheaten is easier than with many breeds since you have a beard to grab onto. Be thorough, make sure to reach all the back molars, and don't forget to praise! Tooth brushing is another practice best done while your dog is secured on a grooming table.

Regardless of whether you will be trimming your Wheaten yourself or sending him to a professional groomer, there are a few things you might want to do yourself. The hair that grows between the pads of his feet can become filthy and will form tightly felted mats. This eventually will cause pain while walking. Before the hair can get to this point, cut it all away with a pair of blunt-nosed scissors or baby nail scissors. Your Wheaten will love the final result as much as you love a pedicure! And you will love his clean feet and even cleaner floor. On the subject of cleanliness, you might also want to use your blunt-nosed scissors to shorten the hair around the anus and, for the girls, the vulva.

Complete Grooming Instructions

Taking on the task of trimming your Wheaten Terrier yourself can seem daunting. Indeed, many Wheaten owners prefer to rely upon the expertise of a professional groomer. But, if you are so inclined and are blessed (or perhaps cursed) with a discerning eye, you will probably do a better job than a professional in turning out a Wheaten Terrier with its distinctive look. This is simply because a professional groomer does not have the time required to create a properly "put-down" Wheaten Terrier. The majority of professional groomers have in their repertoire a generic, all-purpose "Terrier" trim. This trim most closely resembles a Schnauzer. Or, if perhaps you have your own idea of how you want your dog to look, most professional groomers will happily oblige.

This author has seen Wheaten Terriers trimmed like Cocker Spaniels. While there's nothing inherently wrong with this, it does beg the question, "If you wanted a dog that looks like a Cocker Spaniel, why didn't you just get a Cocker Spaniel?" Whatever the case, a professional groomer will generally ensure that your Wheaten Terrier is clean, smells wonderful, has his nails cut, and is neatly clipped from stem to stern and top to bottom. You may even see a bow in the dog's hair—blue if it's a boy, pink if it's a girl. However, if you want your Wheaten Terrier to truly look like one, you have two choices. You will have to find a breeder who shows dogs and takes on clients for grooming, or you must learn to trim your Wheaten yourself.

Trimming Your Own Wheaten Terrier

Regardless of which you choose, both types of trim are labor intensive, with the show trim slightly more so. But once you see how beautiful your dog looks, you may find the effort well worth it! In addition to the supplies mentioned earlier in this chapter, you'll need the combined use of single-edged thinning shears (Economy 44-20 Taper Fine Thinning Shear, or similar), straight shears (such as the Master Grooming Titanium Straight Grooming Shear), and a set of dog clippers with detachable blades and adjustable combs. Below are the basics of

Chapter Seven: Grooming

trimming your own Wheaten Terrier. If you are considering showing your dog, you will find the following instructions helpful as well. You also might want to seek the guidance and expertise of a breeder who also shows. First of all, never trim a dirty dog. Using your scissors or clippers on a dirty coat will ruin them! Assuming your dog has been freshly bathed, dried, brushed, combed, and his nails clipped back, begin with him standing on a grooming table, head in the noose. If you can, it's a good idea to work in front of a mirror, keeping in mind the look you want to create. Referring to the photo of a well-trimmed Wheaten or to the image in Figure 1 (below), work slowly and remember to take breaks. You'll primarily use thinning shears because they allow you to cut into the dog's

Figure 1. Finding the square

wavy hair with few scissor marks. They also create a softer blending of hair and a more natural look.

Start by creating the basic square outline that is typical of most terriers (Figure 2). With thinning shears pointing down, proceed to thin and closely shorten the coat from the throat latch all the way down the chest to the top of each leg. Then move to the dog's rear and proceed in the same manner, thinning and closely shortening the coat from the back side of the tail, down the rump, and both rear legs to the hock joint. Next, follow the natural contour of the dog, completing the square by trimming the topline (from withers to tail). To do this, backcomb the hair there and proceed to thin and shorten it until it is approximately an inch long. The coat on the front and sides of the tail should also blend with the length of hair on the topline but should be slightly shorter.

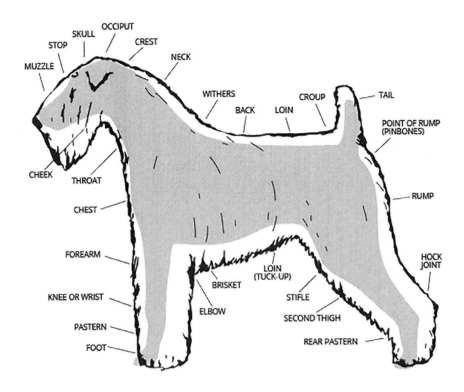

Figure 2. Wheaten side view with points of structure and overlay of coat

Chapter Seven: Grooming

You have now created a rough square outline, and it is your choice where to go from here. You might want to begin shortening the hair on the neck with your thinning shears, starting at the occiput (top of the skull), until it meets with the shorter hair on the topline, allowing the hair length to gradually increase from about one inch on top to about two inches halfway down the neck and meeting the hair on the topline where it should be the same length (one inch) over the withers. Next, blend the hair on each side of the neck, allowing the length to gradually shorten as it meets and mingles with the shorter hair on the throat and down the front of the chest.

Continue in the same manner, blending the coat from the topline down each side of the body, again, with the thinning shears pointed down. If the body coat is excessively thick, start from the bottom and, lifting the coat in layers, slowly tip and thin, combing down as you go, one layer at a time, until you reach the topline. The body coat on each side should gradually lengthen to about one and a half inches. Another method for removing an excessively thick body coat is to backcomb the side coat and, pointing the thinning shears upward, lay them into the coat, close to the skin, and take a couple of swipes in various places. Then, comb the coat down, removing all the hair that you cut out.

It's important to follow the shape of the dog's body when scissoring. The coat should not look like a curtain but rather gently curve, following the contours of the body shape. In the same manner, the dog's natural undercarriage (called the tuck-up) should also be followed and perhaps even enhanced since this gentle curve is aesthetically pleasing. A natural curve on the dog's undercarriage begins at the end of its rib cage and gently arches upward to the point where it meets the hipbone. The space between is the loin. When trimming the side coat and undercarriage, keep in mind that the high point of the curve should be in the middle of the loin and not before. The gentle shaping of this tuck-up is best done with thinning shears as well to maintain a more natural look.

Now to the legs. Standing in front of the dog, think of the legs as neat columns. Comb through one, then pick it up by the paw and give it a couple of shakes. This allows the coat to stand away from the leg. With scissors pointed downward (you can use either thinners or straight scissors here), begin to slowly shorten the hair all the way around, eventually leaving the length at about two inches. Next, with straight shears placed flat against the table and under the hair that is close to the foot, tilt them up slightly so that the outside blade is up while the inside blade is still on the table. Trim the hair from around the foot slightly tighter than the leg hair, retaining the leg's columnar look but with a slightly smaller base. Follow suit with the other front leg.

Moving to the rear legs and using the same procedure with each, backcomb the hair over the hip. Tip and thin the hair so that it matches the body coat in thickness and in length. Continue in the same manner down the leg, at the same time shaping the hair to conform with the bend of the stifle and hock. Now, standing behind the dog, trim the hair tight around the anus but leave sufficient hair on the buttocks so they do not look bare. Continue down the rear of each hind leg, trimming fairly close there and on the inside of each leg as well, taking care to blend the coat gradually into the length of the leg's side hair. Trim around the rear feet in the same manner as the front.

Hopefully, you and the dog have taken some time out several times during this session and definitely before beginning to groom his head. You will be working primarily from the front of the dog. With your clippers, lift each ear flap and shave the hair from the inner flap down to the skin. Then, with the ear still lifted and held between the thumb and forefinger, take your straight shears pointed up toward the tip of the ear and remove all fringe from the ear's perimeter. Use your thumb both as a guide and as a shield to prevent accidentally cutting the ear leather.

Once this is done, trim the hair on the outer earflap. Backcomb the hair on the ear, and with your thinners, shorten the hair almost to the skin at the tip and allow the hair to slowly lengthen until it reaches the top of the ear's natural fold, where it should measure about half an inch. Shorten the hair at the base of the ear and behind the fold as well. The hair at the ear fold should blend slowly with the hair on the top skull, which in turn should blend with the neck coat. With your comb, pull the top skull hair straight up and shorten it with thinning shears to about

Chapter Seven: Grooming

one inch, slowly allowing for a slight curve at each side to blend with the ear fold hair length.

With thinners, tip to about half an inch the hair from the top skull down to a point where the hair wants to fall forward instead of standing up, just prior to the stop (where skull meets muzzle). From there, make sure the remaining hair falls forward, thinning only enough so that it lies flat and still covers the eyes. This is what we refer to as the "fall." There should not be so much thickness that it impedes vision. If it does, thin prudently.

Next, flatten the cheek hair on each side of the head with thinning shears pointing up and thinning/tipping until the hair lies flat and the head looks rectangular. From the side, move to the underjaw, and after combing the hair down, tip with thinners from the throat latch, where the hair should be almost to the skin, slowly lengthening until it meets the beard. Trim the length of the beard to a point so it completes the head's desired rectangular appearance from the side.

The time has come to assess your work! Take your Wheaten off the grooming table and allow him to shake a few times. What do you think? If a few things look amiss, let the dog go for a bit, but not so long that you must start all over with the comb and brush! After a brief respite, put him back up on the table, make the few adjustments necessary, take pride in your beautifully groomed Wheaten Terrier, and let him know how handsome he is!

While the above instructions may seem quite detailed, even more in-depth instructions are available on the breed's national club website (www.scwtca.org/shop). There, you will find, for example, *The Soft Coated Wheaten Terrier Owner's Manual*, with an entire chapter devoted to bathing and trimming the Wheaten Terrier, brimming with illustrative pictures and drawings. Also available is a large grooming chart (handy for hanging on your wall) and a pet grooming pamphlet. These aids are all offered for a nominal fee.

Professional Grooming Services

For a Soft Coated Wheaten Terrier, routine brushing and combing is not simply a basic requirement—it is a necessity. Many owners, however, may not have the facilities for bathing or perhaps have neither the time nor the patience required to groom and trim a dog's coat. Finding a qualified professional grooming service is the logical solution. You most certainly do not want to choose one out of the blue without careful research. Check on the internet for "dog groomers near me." Or ask your vet for a recommendation. If he is reticent to give out recommendations and you have a groomer in mind, ask your vet if he has ever treated any problems on dogs being groomed by them. Ask your dog-owning friends and neighbors for a recommendation. Every time a dog walks out of a grooming parlor, it is a walking advertisement. Dog owners are generally quite chatty, especially if their dog is the same breed as yours!

Once you have narrowed the search down, interview the potential groomers. Some states require that dog groomers be licensed and certified. Ask for proof of certification. Ask if they are members of the National Dog Groomers of America Association. Ask for references from existing clients. You should also ask if you can tour the facility before bringing in your dog. A reputable groomer should welcome a facility tour. If they balk at this, you should probably cross them off your list. Ask if the groomer you are interviewing will actually be the person grooming your Wheaten or if there is a possibility he might be handed off to someone else. It is important to make certain your dog will be handled gently and with great care by a true professional groomer.

While on your tour, pay attention to how clean and well-lit the grooming areas are, whether the cages offer plenty of room for dogs to move about comfortably, how friendly the staff is, and how gentle they are with their charges. While you're there, check to make sure that pets left under blow-dryers are monitored regularly to prevent getting overheated, and ask about what kinds of records the groomer keeps. Ideally, they'll not only keep grooming records but also medical and vaccination records and emergency contact info.

Another option would be a mobile groomer that will come to your home and provide one-on-one grooming. These mini grooming facilities

Chapter Seven: Grooming

FUN FACT
Breed Popularity

The AKC first recognized Soft Coated Wheaten Terriers in 1973. As of 2023, this charming breed is ranked 66th most popular among 284 dog breeds registered with the AKC.

generally operate out of a van or trailer. They typically contain all the tools and equipment you'd find at a standard salon but are designed to work on one dog at a time, right there in your driveway. A big advantage offered by mobile groomers, apart from the convenience factor, is that the groomer can give your dog exclusive attention in a calm setting that doesn't include spending time in a cage or having to deal with unfamiliar noises or other dogs.

Finally, when making your choice, trust your instincts about the groomer. Are you comfortable talking to her and asking questions, or does she seem rushed, distracted, disorganized, or impatient? How does she interact with clients, dogs, and fellow workers? If you feel uneasy about any of it, walk away. Whatever your choice: DIY, grooming salon, or mobile groomer—you want your Wheaten Terrier to look his very best. He deserves it!

CHAPTER EIGHT

Socializing and Doggy Day Care

How often have we heard the new owner of a rescue dog explain away shy and timid behavior by saying, "He was obviously abused"? While such justification may well be true, more often than not, shy, timid, and even aggressive behavior can be attributed to the fact that the dog was never properly socialized. It is rare if ever, that puppy mill breeders take the time to socialize puppies since their motivation is strictly monetary. Puppies are generally kept in pens with their dam and litter mates until money exchanges hands, at which point they are thrust out into a world about which they know nothing. Often, this is the case with backyard breeders as well, typically the result of ignorance rather than lack of concern. Reputable, dedicated hobby breeders, on the other hand, are fully aware that proper socialization is one of the more important underpinnings of a well-bred dog. But something else comes into play as well: the breeder's reputation is at stake, and this they both guard and cherish.

Whatever your puppy's early socializing experience or lack thereof, it now becomes your responsibility. As a start, take advantage of things in close proximity, such as various floor surfaces, carpeting, grass, gravel, dirt, and a variety of sounds. You can gradually expose your puppy to all of the above, plus the washing machine and dishwasher, the vacuum cleaner, the whirr of a food processor, children yelling, and the blacktop road in front of your home. A word of warning about the latter, however. Pay attention to the temperature, especially in the summer months when pavement can become too hot for paws to handle. You will want to acquaint your puppy with as many sounds,

Chapter Eight: Socializing and Doggy Day Care

surfaces, people, places, and objects as possible. Introduce him to people with disabilities, to different races, and, if you live in the city, to the often deafening noise of traffic.

If your puppy becomes frightened in a particular situation, immediately separate him

from it, but don't give up. Say, for example, that your puppy hides in fear when you turn on the vacuum cleaner. Stop the vacuum, put it away for the day, and bring it out the next day without turning it on. Encourage your puppy to play with you near the vacuum; let him sniff it out and investigate it on his own terms, and when he seems fully comfortable around the vacuum, turn it on briefly.

Above all, don't force your pup into any interaction or situation. Pushing him to do something he's not ready for can be very frightening, the exact opposite of what you're striving for. And don't forget the importance of positive reinforcement through praise when your puppy reacts favorably to a situation.

Socializing Your Wheaten with Other Dogs and Animals

> *Socializing should only be done under direct supervision and only with animals that you know. I do not particularly like dog parks because you never know what type of dog is going to be there or how well behaved they are. People tend to assume that all dogs are nice and well socialized, but that's not always the case. Also, you don't know if they've been fully vaccinated.*
>
> DENISE BENDELEWSKI
> *Dhowden Soft-Coated Wheaten Terriers*

Wheaten Terrier puppies are quite friendly and eager to play with almost anything that has four legs. While play with other puppies will usually run smoothly, care must be taken when meeting bigger, older dogs as they can often play too roughly, frightening your youngster. The same holds true when introducing your puppy to any larger four-legged creatures. Such introductions should be cautious, gradual, and made in a very controlled manner, beginning from a distance and slowly allowing closer contact. Positive signs are a lot of sniffing, fast tail wagging, and play bows.

In the case of another older and unfamiliar dog, if your puppy acts frightened or the other dog is growling, trying to retreat, getting its hackles up, or curling its lip, calmly pull back and leave the scene. Never allow your Wheaten puppy to approach another dog closely without requesting permission from the dog's owner. Also, never assume! Some dogs feel threatened by unfamiliar dogs and can become quite aggressive toward them as a defense mechanism. In the case of large animals like cattle or horses, safety must always be at the forefront. Remember that such animals can truly be perilous. One kick can be a death knell.

Remember that the Wheaten is a terrier. Most terriers have built into their DNA a propensity to hunt small critters. Consequently, encouraging

Chapter Eight: Socializing and Doggy Day Care

a friendship between your Wheaten Terrier and, say, a small Chihuahua, guinea pig, or kitten must, once again, be done with caution and in a very controlled environment until you are totally confident that their friendship has been sealed.

Socializing Your Wheaten with People and Children

On the one hand, Wheaten Terriers have a reputation for being somewhat fickle. They tend to love the person they are with, and this is why a well-adjusted adult Wheaten Terrier is generally quite amenable to rehoming. But on the other hand, this does not mean that your Wheaten puppy will automatically take to anyone without a little effort on your part. So, it's important that you make the effort to introduce him to as many people of both sexes and as many generational and ethnic groups as possible. Introduce him to old people in wheelchairs or with walkers, wearing hats or sunglasses.

If there are no small children in your home, it's a safe bet that your Wheaten puppy will find such a meeting intimidating, especially if the child is boisterous with a high-pitched voice and quick to move. It's a good idea to expose a puppy to this sort of scene as often as possible and early on, so that he becomes accustomed to it. Your puppy must never be allowed to chase children, jump up on children, or nip at them! Be clear when you say a firm "NO" and immediately redirect him to acceptable behavior. You may even want to remove the puppy from the scene entirely until he settles down, at which point you can give it another try.

Meanwhile, take the time to teach children, whether yours or others, the importance of respecting their canine friends. For example, children should be taught to always ask if it's okay to pet a dog, whether it's yours or someone else's. They should also be told to speak softly and to pet the dog calmly and gently. Children and dogs belong together so long as they have been taught mutual respect. There is nothing more tragic than to see this bond broken by a bite that could have been prevented.

Chapter Eight: Socializing and Doggy Day Care

If you are the new owner of an older rescue Wheaten and unsure of its background, make a serious effort to establish that he is comfortable with all members of the family and does not show significant attachment to any one person. Such favoritism can easily grow into jealousy or over-protection of the favored person, and this protectiveness may in turn cause an unprovoked attack. A case in point is a couple whose dog becomes overly attached to the wife and, in time, determines that her husband is a threat to her. Eventually, the dog decides to attack him. This scenario happens more than is acknowledged.

However, the typical Soft Coated Wheaten Terrier is, with few exceptions, a happy, friendly dog with, of course, the caveat that he has been well socialized. The worst thing you can do is to keep him closed up in the house. Therefore, feel free, within reason, to take your puppy to lots of different places. Put him in the shopping cart at Home Depot. Walk him around the parking lot or the shopping mall. Use common sense and consider dog parks and other places where multiple dogs congregate, whether on or off leash, off-limits until your Wheaten is a bit older, if at all.

Interaction with people is an inevitable part of your Wheaten's life, so it's important that friendliness on your puppy's part is encouraged. At the same time, never allow people to force themselves on him, especially if he appears frightened or intimidated. You have a responsibility to be his protector under such conditions. Speak up and kindly but firmly request that the person give your puppy space. Perhaps you might suggest that the person calmly offer your puppy a treat.

On the other hand, many Wheaten puppies are bouncing balls of friendly energy and, as such, feed off the excitement of others upon seeing a cute puppy. It's fine to ask excited people to please speak and act in a calm fashion. Remember your puppy's manners should always be enforced, especially in such situations. Do not encourage or allow him to jump up on people. Do not allow him to mouth anyone, either. If you remain calm with a nonchalant attitude, chances are that your puppy will follow suit. A good rule is no petting or other overt attention until your puppy has all four feet on the ground.

Puppy Socialization Classes

> *The use of a professional trainer can save a situation from developing. However, never use a professional trainer without inserting yourself into the equation. You are the one who needs training, and your training plan needs to be established well before the pup comes to your home. Oftentimes training goes awry when humans fail their pets. Rarely are there bad dogs out there, only ill-prepared people.*
>
> SHARI BOYD
> *ARAN*

The puppy kindergarten idea was first developed by Ian Dunbar, a British veterinarian. A renowned animal behaviorist, he is one of the world's most respected experts on dog training and behavior. He designed and taught the first off-leash puppy socialization and training classes, his ideas revolutionizing the world of dog training by putting the emphasis where it belonged—on puppyhood. His methods are fun, easy, and effective, beginning with the use of positive reinforcement and lure-reward training.

Most new puppy owners expect to enroll in some sort of puppy socialization/training class. A class of this sort should never be chosen as a replacement for your personal socialization program but rather as an adjunct activity. These types of classes go by different names: puppy kindergarten, puppy preschool, or puppy training class. Just as with choosing a grooming establishment, choose a puppy class wisely and carefully. Ask for recommendations from your breeder, your veterinarian, and doggy friends. Establish that the class instructors are qualified professionals with appropriate education and are certified in "force-free" training. Titles like APDT, CPDT-KA, KPA-CTP, IAABC, and CTC indicate that your instructor has been certified through a reputable organization and

Chapter Eight: Socializing and Doggy Day Care

is working with current, science-backed information about canine behavior and learning.

It's also a good idea to observe a class in person before signing up. This provides an opportunity to meet the instructor, ask any questions you might have, and provide confidence that the class is a good fit for you and your Wheaten puppy. You want to look for a class with multiple instructors or assistants to ensure your puppy gets one-on-one time. The common ratio in well-run classes is generally two to five puppies per instructor.

Since a puppy's critical socialization window is between six to 16 weeks of age, your puppy will be joining the class before his vaccinations are complete. So, it's critical that the instructor of your chosen class ask all participants for proof of current vaccinations (and perhaps a negative fecal test as well). They should not allow any puppy to join that is showing signs of illness without consulting a veterinarian.

Photo Courtesy of Gay Dunlap

Look for a class that demands the floors be cleaned with a special anti-distemper and anti-parvo solution just prior to the start of class and that no dogs are allowed in the class unless they are participants. Vaccination records should be produced before any puppy is allowed entry. You should always carry your puppy into the classroom. You can also request that the trainer have human class participants remove their shoes before entering the classroom.

Using a Professional Trainer

> *A trend I've seen in recent years is owners who believe all behaviors can be solved with a boot camp or board-and-train-type training program. Many times, this training is viewed as a solution to negative behaviors which have developed over time, and it's believed this training will be a cure-all for those problems. Board-and-train programs usually employ strong negative reinforcement, such as e-collars. Wheatens want to please and do best with positive, consistent training. Using intimidation, punishment, and shock collars will make only serve to make a Wheaten fearful and untrusting. Over time this fear can turn into a dog who is unpredictable and dangerous.*
>
> DEBORAH VAN DE VEN
> *Bradberry Soft-Coated Wheaten Terriers*

Often, the use of a professional trainer is a last-ditch effort to reel in an ill-behaved puppy or adult dog with serious behavior problems when all else has failed. If this is the case, the best course of action is to have the situation evaluated by an animal behaviorist or professional trainer who specializes in these sorts of cases. The best use of a professional trainer, however, is as an accessory to one's own training program. Even the most prepared owner can run into stumbling blocks. Don't be afraid to recognize and admit problems before they become insurmountable. Seek advice from a qualified professional as close to the onset of the issue as possible. Understand the professional trainer's job most often is training the owner as much as training the puppy.

It's important to know that anyone can call themselves a "dog trainer." All it takes is to print up a business card that says so. When choosing a professional trainer, make certain that they have been certified by the Council for Professional Dog Trainers and belong to a professional organization such as the Association of Professional Dog Trainers. Next,

Chapter Eight: Socializing and Doggy Day Care

confirm that their training method utilizes positive reinforcement. The Soft Coated Wheaten Terrier will not respond favorably to harsh or punitive correction.

Canine Good Citizen (CGC)

The Canine Good Citizen program was designed and developed in the late 1980s by the AKC. It encourages owners to be responsible pet owners and dogs to be well-mannered. The program not only teaches dogs good manners but rehabilitates dogs with behavioral issues and is a prerequisite for therapy dogs. Many shelters use the program as confirmation that their rescue dogs are well-behaved. Another program developed by the AKC is STAR, an acronym for Socialization, Training, Activity, and Responsibility. Although there is no minimum age requirement for passing the CGC Test, if your puppy is less than a year old and has not attended puppy kindergarten, STAR is designed to fill the gap and prepare the puppy for taking the CGC test. The CGC test requires that the puppy/dog successfully master all 10 of the following skills before it can receive its CGC designation or title and certificate:

- Remain calm while a stranger approaches and stops to talk to the dog's owner.
- Remain calm while a stranger pets the dog.
- Accept being handled in a manner similar to the way a groomer or veterinarian would handle the dog for grooming or an exam.
- Walk on a loose leash without pulling or lunging.
- Remain calm and walk on a loose leash through a crowd.
- Respond to sit, down, and stay commands.
- Come when called.
- Remain calm as another dog and handler approach.
- Remain calm when distractions such as loud noises are presented.
- Remain calm while the owner hands the dog's leash to someone else and walks away.

If a dog fails to complete even one of the skills, it fails the entire test. Many dog trainers offer CGC classes that prepare you and your dog for the test. Once you feel confident that your dog can successfully accomplish these 10 skills and is ready for testing, you can find a list of local evaluators on AKC's website. And, by the way, the fee is nominal. Although you want to be well-prepared for passing this 10-part test, it is comforting to know that there is no limit to the number of times it can be retaken.

Benefits of a Doggy Day Care Facility and How to Choose One

For starters, doggy day care facilities are not all created equal. This can make choosing the right one for your Wheaten somewhat labor intensive. First of all, let's examine the need for your pup to join one in the first place. Perhaps you spend most of each weekday away from home, your children are at school each day as well, and you have concerns about the dog being at home alone. While these concerns are certainly legitimate, not all dogs react negatively in this sort of environment. On the other hand, if your pup is the energetic sort, doggy day care is a great way to provide him with the opportunity to burn off excess energy and stay entertained.

Your pup will, in all probability, be in one of two day-care environments: a playgroup or a kennel/run situation. It is up to you to decide if your pup is the outgoing type that loves to play with other dogs or if he would prefer to be left alone or perhaps spend brief times with a playmate or two. Many doggy day care facilities just let the dogs do what they want with little interference other than to intervene if there is aggression. A huge room with a cement floor or fake grass and no sniffing or enrichment opportunities with dogs running wild is a recipe for disaster. That is not what I would want for my dog. Supervised play with toys, perhaps some agility equipment and interesting fun activities interspersed with rest time would be ideal for most dogs.

Above all, you want to make certain that your dog is going to be happy with the facility you have chosen. A good place to start is on the internet. Do a search for doggy day cares in your area. If taking your pup and picking him up will be part of your daily routine, it only makes sense

Chapter Eight: Socializing and Doggy Day Care

to keep your travel time to a minimum and find a place close by. When you find a day care that looks promising, make an appointment to tour the facility. Look for good ventilation, solid fencing, safe floor surfaces, and an area where dogs can acclimate before entering the main play area. Notice if the dogs are separated by size and age, by temperament and play style, or perhaps both. If not, you should continue your search.

Ask about the ratio of dogs to staff. The accepted ratio considers 15 dogs to one human a safe one, but allowances should be made depending on the activity level of the dogs. More active dogs require more supervisors, while less active ones may require fewer. Is there a structure to play periods, or is it an all-day free-for-all? Question the staff's training. They should have experience working with and training dogs and be able to enforce/ensure a safe environment, which also means being prepared to handle scuffles if they should break out. Make certain they have a plan for emergency care and are equipped to safely and correctly administer first aid in case of an injury. This in no way implies they should anticipate injuries or accidents but rather that they are prepared in case one occurs.

Hopefully, your Wheaten Terrier is cut out for doggy day care life. Not all dogs are, but if your dog has been well-socialized, he should adjust well to the environment. Still, the day care facility you are considering should require a trial run and temperament test to make sure he is suited to it.

Your choice should leave you feeling confident that you've made the right one. Then, pay attention to how your little one behaves once he is home. If he seems relaxed and a little tired, he's probably in good hands.

HELPFUL TIP
Do Wheatens Make Good Therapy Dogs?

Wheaten terriers are excellent family dogs with affectionate dispositions. But do these lifelong puppies make good therapy dogs? The answer depends on your dog and your patience for training. Wheatens are generally intelligent dogs capable of learning complex commands but are also willful, making them more challenging to train. Still, with patience and dedication, your Wheaten could also be a good fit for therapeutic settings.

Dog Parks

While it's true that dog parks provide opportunities for exercise and socialization, especially if you are worried that your pup has been cooped up all day, the dynamics can present serious problems. For example:

1. Some dog owners, or their surrogates, are not attentive to their dogs, choosing instead to schmooze with other humans or become lost in their mobile devices.
2. Many people let their dogs loose, expecting them to play safely and fairly with other dogs. They have no knowledge of the difference between play behavior and aggressive behavior.
3. If the park has no rules in place, and many of them don't, it exposes your dog to diseases and parasites.
4. Although dog parks ask that owners pick up after their dogs, many even offering free poop bag dispensers for that purpose, there are those that don't comply.
5. If your dog is frequently exposed to aggressive behavior in a dog park, he can easily pick up such behavior and bring it home.

If you happen to live in a smaller community that offers its own "private" dog park, and you are considering taking your dog there, understand that the same problems listed above may exist there as well. The difference may be that these are your neighbors, and you may already be familiar with them and their dogs. Whatever the circumstances, it is always wise to test the waters. Make certain the park is well maintained, with the grass frequently mowed, fencing kept in good repair, and gates secure. Are the owners attentive to their dogs, or are they busily chatting with one another? If owners are oblivious to inappropriate behavior such as mounting, bullying, or aggression, it is not a healthy atmosphere for your dog.

Also, do not assume your Wheaten will love romping freely with a bunch of strange dogs. One of mine hated it and spent the entire time sitting by the gate giving me the stink-eye while my other dog played fetch. Evaluate your dog carefully and honestly before making dog park visits a routine event. Keeping your dog on a leash initially may be a sensible and more conservative approach, but only if he is kept close to you.

Chapter Eight: Socializing and Doggy Day Care

The Dangers of Retractable Leashes

Retractable leashes, quite popular of late, can quickly become hazardous and are considered extremely dangerous for many reasons. Though they allow for more freedom, the owner quickly loses control of the dog when it reaches the end of the leash. The leashes can also readily snap under pressure from a good-sized dog lunging forward. It's easy for another dog or the dog walker to become tangled in them, causing serious injury, burns, cuts, and even amputation. Dogs have also received terrible injuries as a result of the sudden jerk on their neck that occurs when they run out the leash, including neck wounds, lacerated tracheas, and injuries to the spine. Retractable leashes also allow dogs more freedom to continue pulling when they reach the end of the line, and this can look like aggression to another dog who may decide to fight back.

Bottom line: Use only a standard six-foot-length leash attached to a rolled leather collar. Always remain in control of your Wheaten, at the same time giving him the assurance that you are his protector. He wants to feel certain that nothing bad will happen to him because you are there.

Remember, there are alternatives to dog parks! One idea is to create your own playgroup in a private fenced yard with friends whose dogs you know are compatible with each other.

CHAPTER NINE

Dealing with Unwanted Behavior

Hard as we may try to keep unwanted behavior at bay, sometimes a trait simply creeps up on us. That, or else it's a behavior that we once thought endearing until suddenly it wasn't. If your Wheaten Terrier is behaving in a manner that you now find bothersome, annoying, worrisome, or even disgusting, it's never too late to change things.

Jumping

Although this behavior is hardly limited to the Soft Coated Wheaten Terrier, they do seem to have a proclivity for it. This is probably due to their instinctively friendly, joyful manner. As mentioned earlier in this book, many Wheaten breeders and owners have dubbed jumping up on people the "Wheaten Greetin'." While it may seem cute in a puppy, even the most ardent dog lover does not appreciate being body slammed by a 30-to-40-pound dog. Unknowingly, we have encouraged the behavior ever since our puppy excitedly greeted us at the door and we allowed his front feet and legs to leave the ground. The term "four-on-the-floor" is not just reserved for motor vehicles or a drum beat in 4/4 time. Excessive jumping and twirling can lead to serious back and neck injuries as our Wheatens age.

The rules must now change. It can't be an either-or, nor can it be a sometimes-it's-okay, sometimes-it's-not deal. Not allowing paws on furniture or on people must be an uncompromising rule. You can't allow your Wheaten to jump up on you one day and then chastise him for doing it the next. These are mixed signals that only serve to confuse him and in

Chapter Nine: Dealing with Unwanted Behavior

no way convey your expectations. Words won't do it either. "Down" or "off" are meaningless unless accompanied by action. When you push your dog off you, to his mind, this is encouragement since you are touching him, and he sees this as a reward. Everyone in your family, and in fact, every person who comes in contact with your dog, must follow these rules. In other words, it's not okay for him to jump on anyone!

So, how do we break the chain? By refusing to pay attention. As soon as he jumps on you, immediately turn your back. Do not touch him, speak to him, or look at him. Wait until there is a moment where all four feet are on the ground and then quickly reward him. The reward can take many forms—quick praise, a pat, or a treat. The minute your dog starts to jump on you again, repeat the exercise, turning your back to him. At some point in the repetition, he will understand what is expected of him and voila—no more jumping!

Remember the "all-or-nothing" rule. If he can't jump up on you, he can't jump up on anyone else. Before company arrives, secure your Wheaten in another room, in his crate, or tether him on a leash. Assuming your guest is willing to be part of the training, open the door and invite the guest in. If your dog jumps up, say "No," and walk him away. Once he calms down, try again. Keep repeating and remember to reward him with praise or pets and attention when he keeps four paws on the floor.

Another adjunct method is to utilize your earlier training of "Sit" and replace the negative of "No jump" with a positive, "Sit!" He can't both sit and jump at the same time. In other words, you are telling him what TO do instead of what NOT to do. Breaking the cycle of jumping up takes patience, but it can be done.

Chewing

Chewing is a natural and healthy activity for all dogs. It is jaw-strengthening and keeps your Wheaten puppy's teeth clean. You just need to make certain he is chewing on his own things and not yours! Make certain that your puppy does not have access to things that he might find appealing. And with a young pup, that's just about anything that will fit into his mouth. It could be the edge of your living room rug, one of your favorite slippers, or your child's mitten. It is your responsibility to keep all such things out of your dog's reach and make certain he has plenty of his own chew toys. Be sure to pick up your kid's toys, all shoes, and, in short, everything you don't want the puppy to have. Do not give him one of your old worn-out slippers to chew on if you don't want him chewing on people's slippers or shoes! If you find him chewing on a piece of furniture

Chapter Nine: Dealing with Unwanted Behavior

or your living room rug, say a firm "no!" or a strong "ahh ahh" and remove him from the scene. If it happens repeatedly, apply bitter spray. The revolting taste will deter him from returning to the scene of the crime.

Barking

Barking is not always a bad thing. It is one of a dog's ways of communicating. We would welcome our dog barking, for example, if there were an intruder, if our house were on fire, or if one of our children were injured and in need of help. It's the excessive, nonstop barking for no apparent reason that we want to quell. Such behavior is not only annoying to us, but our neighbors are annoyed by it as well. Above all, it's important not to let it go on and on since the longer it's allowed, the more ingrained it becomes.

First, we need to determine why a dog is barking. Often, he wants your attention. After establishing that his need for your attention is nothing dire, simply ignore him by turning your back. Let's assume he is barking to be fed. Even if it's his normal feeding time, turn your back, ignore him, and refuse to feed until he is quiet. Never shout or yell at him. This only stimulates him to bark more because he thinks you are joining in. Train your Wheaten to understand the word "quiet" and use it in a calm, firm voice. Repeat it over and over until he stops, even if it's just for a breath, and immediately give him a treat.

Alternatively, you can teach your dog to "speak." Once he is doing it reliably, signal him to stop barking using the command "quiet" while holding your finger to your lips. Interestingly, dogs often pick up body signals faster than voice commands. Practice these commands when the dog is calm, and in time, he should learn to stop barking at your command.

Keeping your Wheaten well exercised, both mentally and physically, will help as well. A tired dog is a quiet dog. Barking usually gives him an adrenaline rush, something that a tired dog is not interested in experiencing.

Barking at the sound of the doorbell ringing is best dealt with in much the same manner as jumping up on guests. Decide upon a spot within eyesight of the front door but not too close to it. Train your Wheaten to go there and stay, but don't open the door yet. Use lots of rewards and praise. Once he does this reliably, start opening the door while he is in "his" spot. Then, begin to have someone come through the door. Your dog will probably break the first few times, but with patience and practice, he will learn to stay in his spot when the door opens and guests come in.

Incessant barking while you are gone, usually reported by an unhappy neighbor, is generally due to boredom and loneliness. Once again, make certain your dog has been well exercised before you leave him alone. Providing him with several food-dispensing toys, which come in a variety of shapes and sizes, will keep him busy for hours, after which he will no doubt take a nap.

Separation Anxiety

There are breeds known to be particularly predisposed to separation anxiety. Fortunately, the Soft Coated Wheaten Terrier is not one of them. Nonetheless, it can happen. Dogs, in general, are highly social and thrive on human companionship. Consequently, leaving them alone and isolated for extended periods of time can leave them confused and unhappy, and, as a result, they often go into panic mode. This can lead to such destructive behavior as tearing up furniture or pillows. Some dogs have gone so far as to claw and chew right through a wall. Excessive barking is another way in which dogs deal with anxiety. Wheaten Terriers are prone to be more self-destructive, chewing their leg hair off.

It's possible to unintentionally create separation anxiety ourselves. When we treat our dog like a baby, we create a toxic dependency by petting him and talking to him all the time, allowing him to follow us all the time, allowing him to be on our lap or at our feet all the time, etc. When we provide no structure or rules, we are basically allowing him to do whatever he wants whenever he wants, and we are setting the stage for him to be a mess when we leave because we haven't prepared him to be strong, resilient, independent, and alone.

Often, the signs of separation anxiety start to manifest prior to your leaving since your actions generally follow a pattern familiar to the dog, such as putting on your coat, picking up a handbag, or grabbing the keys. If he is exhibiting mild to moderate signs, like whining, pacing, trembling, drooling, or panting, perhaps not eating his food, or ripping something apart, the time is now to deal with it. Make certain your departures are calm and matter-of-fact. It's best to say a simple goodbye or hello or to even ignore your dog. Emotional greetings when you leave

Chapter Nine: Dealing with Unwanted Behavior

or return home send a message to your dog that it's a big deal. Reassure your dog that you are not abandoning him every time you leave by practicing leaving and returning. It might start with a brief out the door and in again, then walking outside for a slightly longer time before reentering. Continue to increase the length of time you are gone until he becomes comfortable with it.

As with any unwanted behavior, remember that a tired dog is a contented, less anxious dog. So, make certain he has had sufficient exercise before you leave. It also helps if you make his alone time fun by leaving a special treat that he only gets when you leave—say, a frozen Kong filled with peanut butter or a snack that will take time to eat. Remember that this special treat should only be given to him when you are

> ## HELPFUL TIP
> ### Lifelong Puppies and Separation Anxiety
>
> Wheaten Terriers are known as energetic and playful dogs. This playful nature often lasts far beyond a Wheaten's puppy years. Because these dogs are so active and affectionate, they may be prone to more behavioral problems if their social and physical needs are unmet. A common behavioral problem for these happy-go-lucky dogs is separation anxiety. Some signs that your dog is experiencing separation anxiety include:
>
> - Destructive behaviors, including inappropriate chewing
> - Inappropriate defecation or urination
> - Excessive barking or howling
> - Escaping
>
> Various factors, including a schedule change, residence change, or lack of exercise, can cause separation anxiety. If you suspect your Wheaten is experiencing symptoms of separation anxiety, it's essential to discuss these behaviors with your veterinarian to rule out any underlying medical issues.

going to be gone. It also helps if you assist your dog in becoming comfortable with being away from you by encouraging independent playtime with his toys or puzzle games (there are many available on the internet).

If your lifestyle is such that you and your family are planning to leave your Wheaten Terrier alone all day every day, only spending time with him in the evening, perhaps you should rethink getting a dog. The alternative is to consider doggy day care or hiring a pet sitter/dog walker to come in several times a day.

Humping

Humping is generally considered unpleasant and often cringe-worthy, especially if your dog is humping a guest's leg, and even worse if the guest is not particularly fond of dogs. There are several triggers for this behavior, and many of them are not sexually related. However, it is less apt to happen with neutered or spayed dogs. Generally, puppies that hump each other are doing it in an exploratory way or in order to establish a social hierarchy. In other words, a more dominant male or female may be trying to prove its dominance by mounting littermates. Such behavior may be embarrassing to us, but to them, it's normal and natural. If your dog suddenly starts humping or seems to be doing it when he never did it before, especially if he is suddenly licking around his genitals, there can be an underlying medical cause, and you should consider consulting your vet. Truthfully, humping only becomes a behavioral problem if and when your dog consistently humps people or excessively mounts other dogs. Often, the trigger is stress or overstimulation.

The question becomes how to stop it. Choose a word that is not already being used as a command, like "off" or "stop." As soon as you see him humping, call his name and use the chosen word in a firm and commanding way. Do not sound angry. Your objective is not to frighten him. If he stops, immediately reward him with a treat, a toy, affection, or whatever he likes most, and remove the object he is humping. If it's a person, you might need to remove your dog from the room. But don't do it in a punitive or revengeful manner. Give him a special treat or toy (one that's not "humpable") to play with instead.

Wheaten Terriers generally want to please and should respond well to the suggested methods of correcting this behavior. If not, you will probably need to accept the behavior and avoid situations where humping will be a problem. You'll need to know how to predict humping behavior and avoid it. This may include, but not be limited to, crating your dog or closing him off in another room when entertaining guests, avoiding situations that you know to be stressful or anxiety-producing to your dog, and providing toys that aren't the right size for humping.

Chapter Nine: Dealing with Unwanted Behavior

Nipping and Mouthing

These behaviors are normal in puppies, primarily because this is the way they begin to interact with each other. When one puppy nips another puppy too hard, the puppy being nipped will give a loud yelp, which in turn provides a clear signal to the other dog that it's not okay. Thus, they teach each other what sort of play is appropriate and what is not. When nipping and mouthing involves a human, however, we must intercede. Our skin tears much more easily than that of a puppy. Also, puppy teeth are razor sharp and quite capable of leaving a puncture wound. A quick hand around your Wheaten puppy's muzzle or a gentle grab of his beard and one calm but forceful word, "No!" will get the message across, especially if it is reinforced when you abruptly walk away and stop playing with him. Do not talk to him, touch him, or look at him. After a brief moment, re-engage with him. Repeat the process if he tries to mouth your hand again. He will quickly understand that when he mouths your

hand or nips, all attention and fun stops. As an adjunct to this, you could try offering a stuffed toy four times larger than his head in such a manner that he has no choice but to play with it rather than mouthing your hand!

Rarely, some Wheaten Terriers will show signs of the herding instinct embedded in their DNA. They will go into herding mode by nipping at the heels of children or guests when they are moving. If your Wheaten shows such an inclination, first say "No!" and have the child or person immediately stop. Ask your Wheaten to perform a trick or a sit/stay, thus redirecting his attention. Reward him when he complies. Never let him get away with this behavior. If you sense that the behavioral instinct is strong and think you might enjoy a fun activity with your dog, consider looking into herding trials in your area.

Noise Sensitivity

Wheaten Terriers seem to have a low threshold for noise. This is a difficult area since determining what is causing a dog's noise sensitivity can often be hard to pinpoint. Sometimes, our dogs can hear things we can't, which adds to our frustration. For example, they may hear or sense the coming of a storm long before we do and begin to shake, quiver, pant, or pace for what seems to be no reason at all. Sometimes, I wonder if they can sense a change in atmospheric pressure levels before we can. These are some of the common triggers for noise anxiety:

- Thunderstorms
- Fireworks
- Beeping from timers, smoke alarms, and other types of electronics
- Fire alarms
- Warning sirens, such as tornado sirens
- Ambulances, police cars, or firetrucks
- Low-flying airplanes
- Other dogs barking
- Doorbells
- Gardener and landscaping equipment

Chapter Nine: Dealing with Unwanted Behavior

Often, the noise sensitivity appears gradually and worsens as a dog ages, for no apparent reason, while for others, it begins when they are puppies and never leaves. It's important to understand that our Wheaten pets are very sensitive to our moods. Therefore, if you have a fear of thunder or lightning, your dog may easily pick up on it, thereby developing fearful behavior. If your carbon monoxide detector starts incessantly beeping and it makes you crazy, your dog will probably go into reactive mode as well. I speak from experience with this one. The device started beeping while I was out shopping, and one of my elderly Wheaten Terriers literally tore my Dust Buster off the wall in reactive lunacy. She showed no signs of noise sensitivity prior to that, but her father was renowned for turning into a complete wuss when he heard thunder or lightning.

Noise sensitivity only becomes a problem if it is excessive and interferes with yours and your Wheaten's everyday existence. Let's examine what to do about relieving his overt reaction to whatever causes incessant barking. First of all, yelling *never works*. Your dog just thinks you are joining him when he barks at the doorbell, the mailman, a siren, or any other loud noises. You must think in terms of outsmarting him. Be a trickster. Devise a way to have the doorbell ring, and when you answer it, there's no one there. The same goes for the mailman. As with all training methods, repetition is the key to success. If he barks unceasingly when guests are present, don't just keep yelling at him to stop. Put the dog in his crate before the guests arrive. Make certain he considers the crate his place of refuge, not a trap or in any way punitive. The crate should be in a quiet, safe place away from the room used for entertaining guests, a spot where the dog can neither see nor hear them. And he will need to have toys and treats to keep him company.

If your guests are amenable, bring your Wheaten out on a leash and introduce him. If he doesn't bark, praise him and allow him to approach the guests (with all feet on the floor). Let him visit for a few minutes, so long as he doesn't bark, and then send him back to his crate with continued praise. Repeating this procedure with your guests will, over time, give the dog the information he wants. Dogs like a predictable life, and they want to be clear about the rules.

Now, what to do if your Wheaten Terrier is showing clear signs of fear, such as shaking, shivering, drooling, or clinginess? There can be far more extreme responses, such as panicked running, defecating indoors, or destructive chewing. As heartbreaking as it is to see our beloved Wheaten so upset and anxious, our instinct is to coddle the dog when this is the worst thing we can do. When we try to console the dog, he is most likely to interpret it as having something to be concerned about. Conversely, it will tend to calm the dog if we can act naturally and nonchalant about the situation.

Your Wheaten will be more likely to react negatively to unpredictable or unusual sounds, such as thunder and lightning or fireworks. Without coddling, it's your job to protect him from what frightens him. If the washing machine, dishwasher, or vacuum cleaner sends him into a freak-out, remove him from the scene. Chances are he will still hear it but in a more

Chapter Nine: Dealing with Unwanted Behavior

subdued manner and will eventually grow to accept the sound. There are products on the market that seem to help, such as pressure wraps, often called Thunderjackets, along with heavy crate blankets that help block out the sound.

It's also important to pay attention to your dog's sound sensitivity in order to establish that it is not caused by physical pain. A veterinary consult will help determine whether the behavior is related to pain, some other medical issue, or anxiety. If pain and other medical issues have been ruled out, there are many medications available, but these should be reserved for extreme cases as a last resort and, if possible, with the guidance of a behavioral veterinary specialist.

CHAPTER TEN

Your Wheaten's Health and Nutrition

Maintaining your Wheaten Terrier's health is multifaceted. Assuming that your Wheaten puppy or adult had a good start by virtue of coming from the kennel of an established, reputable, and dedicated hobby breeder, this will mean that the parents were health tested and found clear of genetic disease and structural deformities. If not, the path to a healthy Wheaten Terrier could well be arduous and costly. You should have received proof of parental health testing, along with all testing and veterinary records for the pup. Also included in your puppy packet should be instructions for projected veterinary care and your breeder's recommended dietary plan and preferred food. If these things were not provided, then the next best plan is to discuss medical care with your vet and do your own research regarding diet. The average Soft Coated Wheaten Terrier's life span is between 12 and 15 years, with some living up to 17. It is important to understand, however, that all dog breeds are susceptible to certain diseases, and the Wheaten is no exception.

Health Disorders in Wheatens

Thankfully, well-bred Wheaten Terriers are relatively healthy. This is especially true of Wheatens whose ancestors, up to and including their sire and dam, have been health tested and regularly screened for certain diseases found to be prevalent in the breed. These diseases include but are not limited to hip dysplasia, progressive retinal atrophy (PRA), protein-losing nephropathy (PLN), and degenerative myelopathy (DM).

Chapter Ten: Your Wheaten's Health and Nutrition

Although the Soft Coated Wheaten Terrier Club of America maintains a watchful eye for potential genetic problems, there are some diseases that remain a challenge, such as protein-losing enteropathy (PLE), irritable bowel disease, renal dysplasia, and splenic disease (including hemangiosarcoma). Please note that these diseases are not specific to the Wheaten Terrier. There is ongoing research at various university veterinary institutions across the country and in Europe as well.

In the constantly changing world of canine genetics and growing knowledge with regard to medical care, the best way to stay current with the latest testing and treatments is to check in regularly at http://www.scwtca.org/health/. The club's website makes an effort to remain up to date with all genetic breakthroughs and treatment protocols. At the time of this writing, it is thought to be vitally important that all Wheaten Terriers undergo genetic testing for PLN-associated variant genes. The test is a simple one involving the use of a cheek swab. Instructions for ordering the test can be found on the SCWTCA's club website: https://scwtca.org/health/health-testing/dna-testing/. It is also recommended that the results of this test be entered in the SCWT database, which will be discussed later in this chapter. The following advice goes for all canines: health testing, including blood work and a complete urinalysis, are vital diagnostic tests that should be part of every dog's annual veterinary check-up. It's also good practice to keep a copy of all health tests in your home files. If you are unsure as to what tests are recommended for your Wheaten Terrier, a trusted source of information, once again, is https://scwtca.org/health/health-testing/annual-testing/.

SCWT Database

The SCWTCA Endowment, Inc. owns and operates the website http://www.scwtdb.org/. It was a project with the sole purpose of collecting detailed health and disease information on as many Soft Coated Wheaten Terriers worldwide as possible. It is accessible at no charge to anyone interested in the

Photo Courtesy of Gay Dunlap

breed. The SCWTCA Endowment was established in 2001 by SCWTCA, Inc for the purpose of supporting research related to the health of the Soft Coated Wheaten Terrier. Since then, it has funded and/or provided many important canine grants, proposals, education, and health projects to protect and preserve the Soft Coated Wheaten Terrier. The database provides researchers with a wealth of assistance for approved research projects in the future, while also serving to reduce health problems in the breed.

As the prospective owner of a Soft Coated Wheaten Terrier, you can do your own research. For example, it is possible to input the name of a breeder of, say, a potential puppy. If the breeder's name doesn't come up, you can assume one of two things: either the breeder is not health testing or does not consider it important. Let's say the name does come up. If you know the name of the puppy's dam, you can look her up to establish if she has been health tested and exactly what tests she has had. From there, you can also input the name of the sire to find out whether or not he has been tested. Failure to note any information regarding the puppy's breeder or its lineage is a red flag ... In other words, it's a clear warning to take your search for a puppy elsewhere.

Nutrition

The health and vitality of your Wheaten Terrier depend upon many things, but foremost among them is diet. Although it may seem absurd to mention this, water is one of the most important of the six major classes of nutrients, not only for humans but for dogs as well. Without it, life cannot exist. Between 70 and 80% of a dog's lean body mass is

Chapter Ten: Your Wheaten's Health and Nutrition

Photo Courtesy of Macy Dermer

water. Its many important functions include dissolving and transporting nutrients to the cells; helping to regulate body temperature; breaking down protein, fat, and carbohydrates for digestion; cushioning organs; and flushing waste from the body. Make sure your dog always has free access to clean, fresh water.

In order to sustain life for canines and humans alike, protein, fat, vitamins, minerals, and carbohydrates are also required. Feeding your Wheaten Terrier a vegan or vegetarian diet fails to supply the nutrients mentioned above, all of which are essential for health in canines. Although it's true that some dog owners prepare their pets' meals from scratch, this is not in your pup's best interests either. The idea of cooking for our pets may be very appealing, especially for those who love to cook, and even more so when our puppy sits at our feet and, with pleading eyes, seems to be begging for whatever it is you're preparing. However, there is no evidence to support claims that home-prepared diets are healthier than commercial diets. Despite what you may have read, very few pets actually need to be fed a home-cooked diet for health reasons, and an improperly prepared home-cooked diet can seriously harm your pet's health, especially if it's a growing puppy.

And there's something else—cooking for a pet isn't necessarily as simple as cooking for a human family. Whereas all commercial pet foods must legally meet or exceed certain amounts of nutrients to be marketed as "complete and balanced foods," studies have shown that the vast majority of recipes pet owners design for their pets or obtain from magazines, books, or the internet are deficient in one or more essential nutrients. It's important to understand that these inadequate levels of nutrients may not cause health problems for weeks or even years, until the pet has a serious health problem that may not be easily reversed. Depending upon vitamin and mineral supplements to augment a home-cooked diet will not serve to bring its essential dietary levels up to meet pet food requirements either.

This isn't to say that you should under no circumstances cook for your Wheaten, but rather that to do so is an expensive, labor-intensive chore, and there are other acceptable paths to excellent canine nutrition. It also is not meant to imply that your Wheaten cannot occasionally be treated to "people food" or that the food can't have an occasional additive, such as a bit of steak or some green beans thrown in. The message here is that your pet is better served by a high-quality commercial dog food.

How do we determine what constitutes a high-quality dog food? If we take a brief look at the history of dog food, we find that commercially packaged dog food did not exist until the mid-1800s. Prior to this, dogs primarily lived outdoors and were fed a steady diet of table scraps. They ate things like cabbage, potatoes, and bread crusts—whatever their owners could spare. Sometimes, they were offered bits of knuckle bone or horsemeat if they were lucky to live in a more urban area. The diets of these early domesticated dogs were not given a lot of thought. Many of them were used for jobs like hunting or protecting livestock, and although considered important, they were replaceable and consequently not treated as we treat our pets today.

Milk-Bone was the progenitor of commercial dog food as we have come to know it, but Ken-L Ration became the primary manufacturer of commercial dog food, with a canned wet product containing mostly horsemeat. Their canned dog food garnered 90% of the dog food market

Chapter Ten: Your Wheaten's Health and Nutrition

prior to World War II. Then, when the war broke out and the government began to ration both tin and meat, the pet food industry turned to producing dry dog food. With the emergence of dog biscuits, kibble, and canned horsemeat as basic categories of commercial dog food, the way was paved for the processing of a major new dry formula that combined all three. This new product was called simply "dog meal." Today, the pet food market is huge, leaving many of us, as a consequence, not knowing who to trust or where to turn. We would like to think our veterinarians would have the answer, but most of them are not nutritionists and often are themselves pet food vendors. As a result, their suggestions might easily be self-serving.

Photo Courtesy of Gay Dunlap

Of two things, we can be certain: all commercial dog foods are not created equal, and the cheapest one on the shelf will never serve you well. Cheap dog food is the equivalent of our fast food. An occasional dip into the fast-food world will not harm us as humans, but committing to an entire bag of cheap dog food is a different story. Consider the cost of your Wheaten's daily diet as insurance against dealing with a sick dog and the resulting veterinary bills.

As we have progressed in understanding human nutritional requirements leading to good health, so has our understanding of what is required for our pets as well. Enter "superfoods." Yes, they do exist. They are rich in the compounds considered beneficial for optimal health, whether human or animal. Understand that superfood requirements for canine health differ from that required for humans. On so many levels, we live in an artificial world. As keepers of our pet's health, it is in our and their best interests to research before purchase. New brands of dog food surface on a regular basis. There are several brands that claim to use these superfoods in various forms, from dry kibble to raw, fresh frozen,

HEALTH ALERT
Identifying Addison's Disease

Wheaten Terriers are generally healthy, hardy farm dogs, but these adorable pups may be more prone to developing a handful of specific health problems. One of these issues is Addison's disease, also known as hypoadrenocorticism. This disease causes underproductive adrenal glands, which regulate potassium, sodium, and cortisol levels. Signs of Addison's disease in your Wheaten include:

- Diarrhea
- Vomiting
- Weight loss or loss of appetite
- Lethargy
- Increased thirst or urination
- Blood in stools

Addison's disease can only be diagnosed with a blood test and is treatable with appropriate medication. If you notice any of the above symptoms in your Wheaten, don't hesitate to contact your veterinarian for further analysis.

and freeze-dried food. The Soft Coated Wheaten Terrier is considered to be a medium-sized breed, and therefore, you must also take this into consideration when making your decision about what to feed.

Do your homework. And don't forget to factor in your puppy's treats. Keep in mind that whereas your Wheaten puppy will require two meals a day, as an adult, one meal each day will suffice. The Wheaten Terrier is considered an adult when he reaches a year of age. By 10 months he should do well on a once-a-day feeding schedule. Never feel obligated to let your Wheaten run your life. Feed in the morning or feed in the evening—whatever suits your daily routine.

Above all, keep your Wheaten Terrier trim and at a healthy weight. Obesity is a growing problem in dogs. A study done in 2019 showed that 55.8% of dogs were clinically overweight, which translates to approximately 50 million dogs. In many cases, the culprit lies in snacks and treats. So please factor into your Wheaten's diet the calories from this source as well. The best way to determine the correct amount of food per meal is to follow the dietary instructions that come with the food you have chosen.

A healthy Wheaten puppy will look chunky and fat. This is natural since he needs the extra nutrition to grow. As he reaches his "teens" and beyond, his body shape will clearly announce whether or not he is a healthy weight. His ribs will not be visible but should be easily felt

Chapter Ten: Your Wheaten's Health and Nutrition

with your hands. If you can actually see his ribs or any bony protuberances at all on his torso, he is too thin. His undercarriage should show that his abdomen is slightly tucked up, and, viewed from above, he will show a slight "waist." What if he is too fat? In that case, you will be hard-pressed to feel his ribs over the layer of fat; there will be little or no waist; often, there will be abdominal distension. Though Wheatens are seldom obese, they can be too thin or too fat. So do pay attention to your Wheaten's body shape.

The Importance of Regular Veterinary Visits

By visiting your vet for regular wellness checks, you are allowing him to establish a baseline, meaning that the more often he sees your pup when he's healthy, the more easily he can identify what's wrong when your pup appears sick. Early detection through blood, urine, and stool tests helps to determine and treat issues before they become serious.

Your Wheaten can't tell you when he doesn't feel well. Dogs are quite adept at hiding pain; it is encoded in their DNA as the result of having evolved from the wild. Remember that, in the wild, a sick or diseased animal soon becomes a hunted animal and, from there, a dead animal. This means that by the time you notice something is wrong, it's because the dog is in pain and can no longer hide it. Consequently, we must always be on the lookout for any sign that might indicate a health issue. Regular visits to your vet allow for the detection of subtle clues or small signs that you might miss, such as breathing issues, heart irregularities, eye problems, kidney trouble, fungal infections, poor dental health, and even certain cancers. A veterinarian can also determine if your Wheaten's joints are working properly and if he is over or underweight.

Vaccinations are something we automatically do for our pets without thinking too much about it. Though they are an important aspect of pet care, it's a good idea to understand which ones are necessary as opposed to those that are based on one's lifestyle. Vaccines are separated into two main categories: core and non-core. Core vaccines will protect your Wheaten from diseases that have high fatality rates—those common in the environment that are easily spread between animals or to people, such as rabies, distemper, parvovirus, and hepatitis. Rabies vaccinations are required by law in the mainland United States. Lifestyle vaccinations, also labeled "non-core," are a matter of choice, depending upon the prevalence of the disease organism in your area and the severity of the symptoms. Also to be considered is your Wheaten's day-to-day activity. Is he walked close to wooded areas where wild animals live, or is he in close contact with other dogs, say, at doggy day care? Is he included in a lot of family travel? These are issues best discussed with your vet. If he is an enlightened and up-to-date clinician, he will be concerned with over-vaccinating your Wheaten Terrier, not to mention your pocketbook. As of this writing, the opinion of the AAHA (American Animal Hospital Association) is that adult dog vaccination boosters should be administered every three years.

Depending on where you live, both internal and external parasites can wreak havoc on your pup's health. For example, if mosquitos are prevalent in your area, heartworm is a serious threat since they are spread by mosquitos. It's vitally important to consider a regular heartworm preventative. Your vet may advise you of other ways to mitigate the dangers of heartworm if you live in an area where mosquitos are less common. One way is to keep your Wheaten indoors at dusk and dawn (the hours when mosquitos are most active). Also, if your adult Wheaten is in full coat, the possibility of being bitten by a mosquito is somewhat diminished.

Many of the grooming topics discussed in Chapter 7 of this book are significantly germane to your Wheaten Terrier's health and bear mentioning again. Breeds with hair, as opposed to fur, tend to also produce hair in areas that can create health issues. Make certain that your groomer understands the importance of these issues and, in some instances, that your vet, rather than the groomer, handles the required procedure.

1. Excess hair in the ear canal. This hair, if left to grow unchecked, tends to create an excess of ear wax and can cause ear infections. It is important that this excess hair is removed from time to time.
2. Hair between the footpads. Keeping this area clean, free of hair, and neatly trimmed will ensure that your dog's paw pads remain healthy. Hair left between the pads will eventually form dirty mats, which will cause your dog pain when walking. Keeping the hair short

Chapter Ten: Your Wheaten's Health and Nutrition

will keep your dog's paws clean of debris and excessive mud, dirt, and snow.

3. Keeping nails cut short is important for the health of your Wheaten's feet.
4. Excess hair around the genitals should be removed as a sanitary measure.
5. Anal gland expression is not always necessary, but when it is, by all means, leave the job to your veterinarian. Do not trust a groomer to do it. Meanwhile, make sure your Wheaten is a healthy weight and is eating a diet with enough fiber to firm up stools.

Pet Insurance

Pet insurance works in much the same way as your own medical insurance policy. Given the myriad choices of coverage, your decision will revolve around what you feel your pocketbook will allow and what you might consider a worst-case scenario. If you decide to opt for insurance, it's best to make the decision early in your Wheaten puppy's life because your insurance premiums will generally be less, and most pet insurance policies do not cover pre-existing conditions.

Statistics tell us that four out of five pets will have an unexpected emergency in their lifetime. In the final analysis, opting for pet insurance will offer you peace of mind and certain options such that you can make the best decisions for your Wheaten's health without financial risk. Before shopping around, ask yourself two questions: what are you willing to pay out-of-pocket for vet bills and how would you pay for costly vet expenses if something did occur, like an accident or a serious illness? There are several websites that allow the prospective pet insurance buyer to compare plans and companies. One such site is https://buyersguide.org/pet-insurance/t/dog.

An important component of owning a Soft Coated Wheaten Terrier, or any dog for that matter, is the firm commitment to serving as your pet's health advocate. His health is totally in your hands.

CHAPTER ELEVEN

Your Wheaten as a Show, Performance, or Therapy Dog

Do not assume just because these activities are listed separately that your Soft Coated Wheaten Terrier cannot take part in all three. Many have done just that. The various performance activities are always available, regardless of championship status. Once a dog qualifies as a therapy animal, he may serve in many capacities, including as his owner's personal therapy dog and/or in the public arena by visiting schools, hospitals, hospices, nursing homes, and the like.

Chapter Eleven: Your Wheaten as a Show, Performance, or Therapy Dog

Show Dog/Breeding Stock

> 66
>
> *If you are interested in becoming a breeder, be sure to do your research. Attend specialties. Talk to lots of breeders and exhibitors after the show. Buy a catalog, watch the judging closely, and make notes about dogs that you liked. Contact those owners afterward and show your interest in learning. Finding a breeder who can mentor you in the breed is a very valuable tool. Understanding the dogs behind your show/breeding program hopefully will add to your chances for success. Pay attention, listen, and learn from the breeders who have dedicated years to a successful breeding program.*
>
> SHARI ROBINSON
> *Keepsake Wheatens*
>
> 99

Perhaps your breeder asked if you would consider showing your Wheaten pup in conformation events and/or if you would allow it to be bred. Or maybe you decided on your own that it might be fun to throw your hat into the show ring. If your pup came from a reputable, dedicated hobby breeder, and you weren't asked about interest in showing or breeding, you probably signed a spay/neuter agreement. If this is the case, your Wheaten is ineligible to compete in conformation events, although all other competitive sports are open to him. Exclusion from conformation in no way reflects negatively on any dog but rather reflects the dedication of his breeder to the precept that only dogs of exceptional structural quality be used for procreation.

There is a valid reason for excluding sexually altered dogs from conformation competition. Conformation shows were originally designed as a means to evaluate breeding stock, and since spayed or neutered dogs are not able to procreate, adding them to the mix would muddy the waters. These shows are more than beauty pageants. They involve purebred dogs being judged for conformity to their breed standards and are considered an essential step toward the preservation and improvement of their breed so that future lines remain of high quality. Your Wheaten Terrier may seem perfect to you, and rightly so. However, to be competitive in conformation events, he should embody, or come

Photo Courtesy of John Ashbey Ashbey Photography

Chapter Eleven: Your Wheaten as a Show, Performance, or Therapy Dog

Photo Courtesy of Gay Dunlap

Annie Sullivan and Stephen Dedalus, 1971

close to, the ideal characteristics of the breed as called for in the standard. Breed standards are written descriptions of the ideal physical, functional, and temperament traits of a specific breed. The Soft Coated Wheaten Terrier Standard is available at www.scwtca.org/standard and https://images.akc.org/pdf/breeds/standards/SoftCoatedWheatenTerrier.pdf.

Showing the Soft Coated Wheaten Terrier in conformation requires a serious commitment above and beyond simply placing a show lead around the dog's neck and walking into the ring. First of all, you must either become adept at putting him in a show trim (instructions in Chapter 7), or you must find an experienced groomer who has the know-how. Just any old groomer won't do since most groomers are only equipped to offer what is vaguely labeled a pet trim, one done with clippers. If your breeder has encouraged you to show, chances are she will not only offer to keep your dog in a show trim but will also give you lessons in how your dog must be handled in the show ring. She may want to show him herself, leaving the job of entering the shows and paying the fees up to you. Another avenue open to you is the hiring of a professional handler; however, be forewarned that this can put quite a strain on the pocketbook.

First, you must be certain to register your Wheaten puppy with the AKC (your breeder should have given you a puppy registration form). If the form is marked as "Limited Registration," you must talk to your breeder about changing it to "Full Registration." Reputable hobby breeders choose limited registration in order to discourage the breeding of pet-quality dogs, thus ensuring that only the best in their breeding programs are used for reproduction.

Assuming you have chosen the DIY road, the next step is to contact a kennel club near you and inquire about conformation classes. These classes will teach you how to present your dog in the show ring. Understand that there are no perfect dogs, and with this in mind, the class instructor will teach you how to minimize your Wheaten's faults and maximize his good points. While it's true that professional handlers have the edge when it comes to winning, there is good reason for this. They have made it their business to train, groom, and present their dogs to perfection. Is there a chance for you under these conditions? Absolutely! All you have to do is learn to handle, groom, and present your Wheaten like a professional! Attend dog shows and sit ringside, watching the handlers of Wheaten Terriers, especially the professionals or the owner/handlers who have learned to handle like a pro. They did it, and you can do it too. Your reward is the right to call your dog a champion and to add the coveted prefix "CH" to his name.

Performance Trials with Your Wheaten

Performance in the dog world encompasses a plethora of competitive events, with more being added every year—most recently, fly ball. Taking part in any of these events will provide far more mind/body exercise for your Wheaten Terrier than a dog park or doggy day care. Most

Chapter Eleven: Your Wheaten as a Show, Performance, or Therapy Dog

communities offer training classes in the modalities discussed below. If you are interested and have no success finding one, you might contact the American Kennel Club (www.AKC.org).

Obedience Trials

The granddaddy of all performance competition, obedience trials were first introduced by the AKC in 1933. They were developed as a series of exercises that would demonstrate the dog's usefulness as a companion and to show that the dogs could be trained to always behave at home, in public, and in the company of other dogs. For many years, it was the only dog sport available other than conformation, and it provided an outlet for dog owners to continue with their dogs in a competitive sport beyond the conformation ring. Obedience begins with the basic commands you may have already taught your Wheaten: heel, sit, stay, down, come. Most communities and many local kennel clubs offer classes in

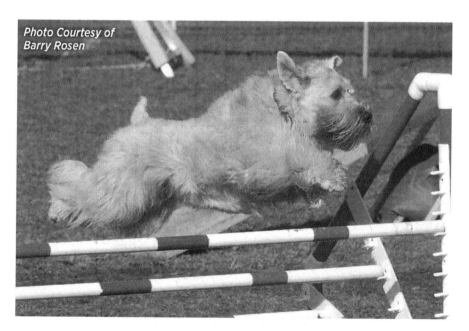

Photo Courtesy of Barry Rosen

canine obedience designed to prepare you for the actual competition. Obedience trials begin with Novice. Companion Dog (CD) is the title awarded to the Novice competitor who successfully completes all the requirements. There are four more levels of competition—Open (CDX), Utility (UD), Utility Excellent (UDX), and the pinnacle of obedience competition, Obedience Trial Champion (OTCH). These titles are shown as a suffix to your dog's name.

Agility Trials

If you've ever considered replacing your personal exercise routine with an activity that includes your Wheaten Terrier, agility may well be the answer. Far beyond exercise, it also reduces boredom, reinforces positive behavior in your Wheaten, and strengthens the bond between the two of you. It is an extremely fast-paced, physically and mentally stimulating challenge for you both. At a typical agility trial, an obstacle course must be completed in a given amount of time and in a predetermined pattern by both dog and handler. For the dog, it involves running, climbing, balancing, jumping, and weaving, all at a fast pace. You, as the handler, must not only give direction but also keep up with the dog. Agility is not suitable for old dogs with health issues or dogs that have been injured, and it can be stressful for dogs that are nervous or anxious. It's also not for puppies, although it's possible to start out gradually, saving the actual competition for when a dog is mature, no earlier than 12 to 18 months. Agility trials also offer titles for levels of competition that are added as a suffix to the dog's name.

CAT and FastCAT

The Coursing Ability Test is considered one of the easiest ways to get involved in the world of dog sports. The idea is patterned after lure coursing, which was devised for sighthounds to test their focus and speed while chasing a lure. CAT was created to give all breeds an opportunity to chase a lure. Lure coursing itself is set up on a circular course 300 yards long. This is a long distance to run, and not all dogs are able to do it. It also requires a lot of open space in which to set up the track. Nonetheless, lure coursing events are still open to mature dogs of all breeds, not just sighthounds. FastCAT is a relatively new sport wherein the dogs chase the lure down a straight 100-yard track. Since the courses are fenced in, your dog is allowed to run free, and, for that brief moment, he is completely consumed by the natural instinct to chase an object in motion, free and unencumbered. The experience is incredibly uplifting for both you and your dog. Dogs must be at least a year old to compete.

Scent Work

Any dog owner has to be aware of the role a dog's nose plays in his life. They are constantly in the throes of sniffing at stuff. A dog has 300 million scent receptors in its nose compared to the mere six million that humans possess. This adds up to 50 times more smelling power than we have. Dogs also have a specialized anatomical structure in their nasal cavity called the olfactory recess. It's a large maze of highly convoluted airways that we humans lack. In dogs, the recess lies right behind the eyes and takes up almost half of the interior of the nose. This allows dogs to sniff odors undetectable by us. Secondly, air travels differently through a dog's nose. When humans inhale, all the air that passes through the nose passes into the lungs, but this isn't the case with dogs. Roughly 14% of the air that dogs take into their body is transported through a series of bony turbinate structures that spread it out over millions of receptors, helping the dog to distinguish the faintest of scents. Lastly, the slits on either side of a dog's nose circulate air in such a way that additional odors are funneled into it, creating a nearly continuous whiff of whatever they are interested in smelling. Scent work, sometimes referred to as nose work, is a sport that is patterned after professional canine detection work, e.g., the search for missing people, such as search and rescue following natural disasters. In this sport, the dog works to locate a missing object that has been scented with an essential oil. The sport is a real confidence builder. It's great fun for both you and your dog and is unique in that your dog is allowed to become the leader. As with all canine sports, most communities offer both training classes and trials in scent work.

Barn Hunt

If there was ever a canine sport designed especially for Wheatens, this is it. As we noted earlier, a Wheaten Terrier's primary function in its country of origin was to rid his master's farm of vermin. Do not be surprised, however, if your Wheaten Terrier chooses to look the other way at a skittering mouse since that strand of DNA seems to have diminished with some Wheatens over time. Barn hunt trials are based upon the traditional roles many dogs, mostly Terriers, played in vermin elimination and provide the opportunity for breeders to test their dogs' working traits and abilities. However, they are also open to any owners who want their

Riley and GCh Gleanngay Runaway CGC RATN

Chapter Eleven: Your Wheaten as a Show, Performance, or Therapy Dog

dogs to play the game so long as the animal can fit through an 18" wide by bale-height tall tunnel. It's an exciting and rewarding sport where you and your dog work as a team to locate and mark rats. The rats are safely held in aerated tubes hidden in a maze of straw or hay bales. If you and your Wheaten Terrier want to give it a try, most communities have local barn hunt clubs that offer beginner events. Taking it still further, it's possible for you and your dog to compete for advancing titles as the courses become more difficult and challenging, with additional obstacles and more rats to discover. For more information, check out the Barn Hunt Association on the internet.

Dock Diving

This performance event probably ranks as the most fun dog sport of all. It is also the most beginner-friendly and exciting. Open to dogs of all breeds, including mixed breeds, the only requirement is that dogs must be at least six months of age on the day of the competition. It is a relatively simple canine sport, and it requires almost no training in order to get started. It can be done by any dog that loves toys and water. There is a downside for the Wheaten Terrier's human family regarding just how willing they are to deal with a sopping wet dog once the fun is over and they face the drive home. Solutions to the dilemma do exist. In the summer months, or when the event is held indoors, a thorough toweling off will ease the problem. A more extreme solution would be to shorten your Wheaten's coat from stem to stern with clippers. The latter suggestion would be best considered after you have determined that this sport is definitely yours and your Wheaten's cup of tea!

There are three disciplines in this sport: distance jump, hydro dash, and air retrieve. Distance jump is the most basic of the three, and it consists of the dog running down a 40-foot-long dock and jumping into a 41-foot-long pool. All three disciplines are scored entirely on the dog's performance. If you think you and your Wheaten Terrier might enjoy this activity, many events offer "try-its," which allow dogs to get their feet wet and become familiar with the event before entering competitively. There are several sanctioning bodies that host dock diving competitions, but the one that holds the most competitive events, including the National Showcase, is North America Diving Dogs. If you are interested in involving your dog in dock diving, visit the North American Diving Dogs website, where you should find a listing of local events, allowing you to get started.

Therapy Dog

It's important to understand the difference between therapy dogs, service dogs, and emotional support dogs. Service dogs, designated so through the American Disabilities Act (ADA), are individually trained to serve people with disabilities. Their work is directly related to the individual's disability, and training is both exacting and specialized. Emotional support dogs are not considered service dogs by the ADA, with their owners having limited legal rights. They are considered companion dogs meant to ease stress, anxiety, depression, and various psychological and emotional disorders.

Therapy dogs play a different role in society. A therapy dog is a pet that accompanies its owner to specific settings for the benefit of the residents or clients in a particular setting or as part of a therapeutic intervention. A therapy dog is trained to provide affection and comfort to people in hospitals, retirement homes, and nursing homes. They can serve the same function in schools, aiding children with learning difficulties and in communities under stressful situations, such as disaster areas. Therapy dogs come in all sizes and breeds.

The most important characteristic of a therapy dog is its temperament. A good therapy dog must be friendly, patient, confident, gentle, and at ease in all situations. Therapy dogs must enjoy human contact and be content to be petted and handled, sometimes clumsily. A therapy dog's primary job is to allow unfamiliar people to make

Chapter Eleven: Your Wheaten as a Show, Performance, or Therapy Dog

physical contact with it and to enjoy that contact. Children, in particular, enjoy hugging animals; adults usually enjoy simply petting the dog. The dog might need to be lifted onto, or climb onto, an individual's lap or bed and sit or lie comfortably there. Studies have shown that interacting with therapy dogs as part of an animal-assisted intervention approach yields both physical and psychological benefits to both humans and the dogs.

Many Wheaten Terriers seem to be quite suited for this work, both physically and mentally. For the most part, when raised well, they are sweet and

> **HELPFUL TIP**
> **Finding a Therapy Dog Training Program**
>
> If you're looking into a therapy dog certification program for your Wheaten Terrier, you'll want to find an organization with national recognition. Most places that employ therapy dogs, such as hospitals, schools, or nursing homes, will look for dogs with rigorous and advanced therapy work training. Affiliation with a therapy dog group recognized by the AKC can help you and your therapy dog get started. In addition, most therapy dog groups can also provide liability insurance for your dog during volunteer engagements. For an up-to-date list of AKC Therapy Dog training and affiliated groups, visit the AKC website.

gentle. Then there's the Wheaten Terrier's physical appearance. Children and adults alike quite often fall in love with this beautiful dog with a soft, silky, hug-worthy coat. Wheatens just naturally look as though they want to be cuddled—or at least petted. They might even send out the vibe that they'd love to sit on a lap. And much to everyone's liking, because your Wheaten doesn't shed, its hair stays where it belongs—on the dog, thus affording little concern over allergies to ruin the day.

Training your Soft Coated Wheaten Terrier as a therapy dog offers you the feel-good opportunity to be of service in your community and provides a sense of well-being to the lives of all involved. If this idea is appealing, you may have already set the wheels in motion by providing your Wheaten Terrier with some basic obedience training along with passing the Canine Good Citizen Test. If not, both would be a prerequisite. Following this, you should join a local therapy dog group where you and your Wheaten will learn additional skills that will serve you both well as volunteers.

CHAPTER TWELVE

Your Aging Wheaten

And so, the days, weeks, months, and, finally, years of precious moments with your Wheaten Terrier have become beautiful memories of joyful times. Almost before you know it, your sweet puppy has passed beyond his teenage years and through adulthood into his golden days as a senior citizen. The love affair has blossomed into something of far greater depth. More than just a pal, he adores you as much as you adore him.

Fortunately, the Soft Coated Wheaten Terrier often retains its youthful vim and vitality far into adulthood. My experience is that a thoughtfully bred, healthy Wheaten will live between 13 and 15 years. Eventually, however, age creeps up, and before you realize it, your Wheaten Terrier has progressed from active adult to elder citizen.

The commonly held belief that one year of a dog's life equals seven years of a human's life is faulty. While a dog at one year may equal a child of seven, after the first year, the changes in a dog's life occur more slowly, so a more reasonable estimate is to add four human years for each year of a dog's life.

The dedicated care we provide our Wheaten Terrier over the years directly correlates with his quality of life as a senior citizen. And it must be mentioned, once again, that if your Wheaten came from a committed, conscientious breeder, one whose breeding stock is routinely health tested, this will also bode well for the dog's longevity and play a role in ensuring that his later years will be golden.

Chapter Twelve: Your Aging Wheaten

Health in The Older Wheaten

Making certain that your Wheaten is healthy and comfortable is key to his well-being. And it's important to take note of any changes in his personality traits or physical habits. A well-bred, well-cared-for Wheaten Terrier may easily reach the age of 10 before showing any serious signs of aging. Such signs may include being slower to get up from a nap, a

Photo Courtesy of Patricia Zurek

HELPFUL TIP
Wheaten Life Expectancy

The average life expectancy of a Soft Coated Wheaten Terrier is around 12 to 15 years. However, some Wheatens have been known to live up to 17 years with the proper veterinary care and genetic predisposition. According to a Wheaten Health Initiative Purebred Dog Health Survey conducted for Soft Coated Wheaten Terriers in 2004, this breed's leading cause of death is cancer, followed by old age.

slight stiffness when walking, apparent hearing loss, or eyes slightly clouding over, generally from nuclear sclerosis or the beginning of cataracts. A note here: reputable breeders register their breeding stock as clear of serious eye disease after a thorough exam by a licensed veterinary ophthalmologist.

Mouth/teeth hygiene must remain an important part of your Wheaten Terrier's regular routine. Tooth brushing from puppyhood on and learning to scale his teeth as part of your grooming ritual while he is still a youngster is an exercise you won't regret. Hopefully, you have made brushing his teeth a regular part of your grooming procedure. Otherwise, bi-yearly trips to the vet for teeth scaling will help ensure healthy teeth and gums. Ignoring dental hygiene could put your dog at risk of developing gingivitis, periodontal disease, bad breath, and, in severe cases, pain, tooth decay, and tooth loss. If you've been lax in this department, it's never too late to start. A regular toothbrush and doggy toothpaste will do the trick. Otherwise, you can wrap a piece of gauze around your finger, add some dog-friendly toothpaste, and gently rub around his teeth and gums, which will get him used to the idea.

Certainly, maintaining proper weight for your Wheaten Terrier is essential for good health, at all ages. But it's all too easy to let your heart rule your head when it comes to dealing with those sad, soulful eyes of your aging Wheaten begging for a treat! It's best to keep the excess fat off in the first place since dieting is never fun for either of you. It's hard to cut back on treats and regular meals once a dog has become accustomed to them. His pleading eyes will bore right through you and create an intense sense of guilt. One way to solve the problem of what appears to be an almost empty dog bowl is to add something noncaloric as a filler. Plain puffed rice cakes may fit the bill, but care must be taken to ensure that

Chapter Twelve: Your Aging Wheaten

they contain nothing that might be considered an allergen. Make certain they are free of added salt, spices, or artificial flavors. A better choice is green beans, so long as they're plain. This low-calorie vegetable is high in fiber, promotes healthy digestion, and offers several other health benefits. However, while green beans can be an effective weight-loss snack, they should never replace your dog's regular meals. Many quality companies offer weight-loss dog food. Just make certain that the one you choose contains superfoods and that they are considered dog friendly.

Make certain your dog's water bowl is always filled with fresh, clean water. The bowl can become quite slimy by the end of the day, so please give it a good cleaning before the refill.

Arthritis, cancer, heart problems, and deteriorating kidney function are within the realm of possibility for all aging canines, including the Soft Coated Wheaten Terrier. Other diseases of age include degenerative myelopathy and age-related intervertebral and cervical disc disease. Dealing with such medical conditions will require veterinarian care.

Assuming your Wheaten Terrier has been well cared for throughout his life, these golden years with him will be a very special time for all. He will love being doted on and begin to enjoy more than ever before the quiet time spent with you and his family.

Adjustments

> *Adjust your expectations regarding exercise and how much you put into the food bowl as your dog ages, but continue routines, just at a slower rate. Dogs do not thrive as exercise decreases while food and treat quantities stay the same.*
>
> EMILY HOLDEN
> *President of the SCWT Club of America*

It's important that you take note of any noticeable changes in your Wheaten's normal behavior and activity, however subtle, and consult with your veterinarian before making any changes in his lifestyle. Many conditions can be made less severe with changes in diet or through medication. As a senior dog, he should be seeing his vet more often than when he was younger. Twice-a-year exams are recommended, at which time the vet will probably want to test the dog's blood and urine for potential signs of metabolic disease.

You may find that he can no longer deal with the lengthy brushing and combing regimen. His inability to stay still or stand for long makes your job more difficult. You may want to consider cutting his coat back with clippers to a length more easily and quickly managed. This shorter hair-do also allows you to check your dog's skin more easily for dryness, inflammation, and potential growths or lesions. Remember to keep his inner ears clean, and don't forget to trim his nails.

An aging Wheaten will sleep more, and you will note that he seems to no longer enjoy the long, brisk walks of his youth. This is all quite natural. Do take him for shortened trips around the neighborhood or longer, more leisurely ones while paying attention to his body language and the cadence of his gait, staying sensitive to any sign that he is tiring and appearing ready to head home. These golden years with your Wheaten Terrier can be the sweetest of all, with the rambunctiousness and playfulness behind him, leaving him with nothing but love and affection to give you.

An adjustment to bathroom breaks may be in order if you find your dog is showing signs of incontinence. Under no circumstances should you consider limiting his access to water. Before making any adjustments, it would be wise to rule out any medical cause other than simply old age. Incontinence can be the result of such conditions as a urinary tract infection, kidney disease, dementia, and even arthritis. Supplements and medications can help treat incontinence, especially if the root cause is a medical issue. Once any medical disorder has been ruled out, it becomes your job to find a solution. If a dog is free to relieve himself by exiting the house through a doggy door, you may find dribbling on the way out. "Belly bands" for males and doggy diapers for bitches are a great solution to the dribbling problem, although, speaking from personal experience,

Chapter Twelve: Your Aging Wheaten

Photo Courtesy of Gay Dunlap

doggy doors are wonderful unless (and until) incontinence hits your dog in its senior years. The problem is that the boys take themselves out the door and do a complete urination into the belly band, and the bitches both urinate and defecate into the diaper.

If he depends upon you for all of his potty breaks, you will probably need to take your dog out with greater frequency. If he sleeps in a crate or in a specific place in your home, you might want to add an incontinence pad to his bedding. Understand that when a dog is truly incontinent, he has no control over his urination, and it can happen before he even realizes it. This, in turn, can cause him to feel shame and even worry about being scolded. Remember to remain patient and understanding. After all, it's not his fault.

Age-related arthritis in an older dog is not uncommon, and if your senior Wheaten is showing signs of this or any other inflammatory joint disease, he may benefit from an orthopedic or heated dog bed.

Deafness, either partial or total, is not unusual in the older Wheaten Terrier, probably due to age-related degeneration in the inner ear, as seen in older people. Often, it is not all that apparent since so much of our communication combines several senses, among them sight, smell, and touch. Dogs are also quite good at reading body language. Deaf dogs tend to "sleep well." Owners of old dogs may notice that they now tolerate the noise of a vacuum cleaner or fireworks when previously they did not. If you are having problems getting your dog to respond to your call, you may want to try a different approach: perhaps a lower pitch to your voice or a clap of your hands.

It's entirely possible at an advanced age that your Wheaten has lost a considerable amount of his eyesight. This is not a good time to be making changes to his environment. In other words, it's best not to move the furniture around or add new items. His comfort level lies in knowing where everything is within his home surroundings.

We have, in recent years, been made aware that dogs, too, can develop dementia. Known as canine cognitive dysfunction, a few signs of this are restlessness, sleepwalking, staring into space, disinterest (e.g., in favorite toys, foods, or people), separation anxiety, and irritability. If you suspect your senior Wheaten Terrier may have CCD, a visit to your veterinarian is a must. There are some diseases that mirror CCD and must be ruled out. Once this is done and CCD has been positively diagnosed, there are diets, supplements, and prescription drugs that can relieve or reduce the dementia symptoms.

Keeping the Mind Alive

Ignore the old adage that you can't teach an old dog new tricks! Just because your Wheaten is old doesn't mean he can't still enjoy life. There are many canine puzzle toys on the market that senior dogs enjoy. Those walks may be shorter, but he will enjoy being allowed to explore at his own pace and sniff to his heart's content. This is called a "sniffari!" Consider taking him to a new neighborhood or to explore a new trail. Give him sufficient time to take in any new sounds or sights. Taking him

Chapter Twelve: Your Aging Wheaten

to a pet-friendly store or coffee shop is a great opportunity for him to enjoy new sights and smells. He might also enjoy being signed up for a scent work class. These are all ways to help stimulate his brain.

If you sense that the days with your Wheaten are drawing to a close, treat him and yourself to the activities you and he have especially enjoyed together. Perhaps it's playing fetch with a ball. If he can no longer chase it, try rolling it to him. If he can no longer walk, try putting him in a baby stroller for a walk in the fresh air. Remember that time is a limited resource, and you can't get more of it once it's gone.

When It's Time to Say Goodbye

There is no more heart-wrenching moment than having to say a final goodbye to your beloved Wheaten Terrier, your best friend. But unfortunately, the time inevitably comes. We all would feel blessed to have our pet leave this earthly plane peacefully and serenely in his sleep, but unfortunately, this is most often not the case. Remember that your Wheaten belongs to a species wherein hiding pain and infirmity is built into the DNA. Also built into his DNA is the knowledge of what must be done when his days are at an end. In the wild, he may separate himself from his family. But this is not possible for our beautiful dog, who has never known life other than as part of a human family. He certainly does not deserve to meet a frightened, bewildering end while lost and alone. Consequently, it becomes our responsibility to decide when enough is enough. The question is, just how do we go about determining this, especially if the dog's body language isn't providing us with clues?

Such was the case with one of my beloved old dogs, Doc. He was just shy of 16, standing absolutely motionless and staring into space, when it suddenly struck me rather intensely that his spirit had left his body. It was as though I was looking at an empty shell. At that moment, I started to cry, picked him up, asked him to forgive me, and together, my husband and I took him to our vet to be euthanized. His body joined his spirit peacefully in my arms, amid many shed tears. I have never really laid to rest the possibility that I waited too long, and I have often thought, better

a day too early than a day too late. Whatever your decision, there will probably be twinges of doubt unless your old dog is obviously suffering and needs your help to ease his suffering. Below are some signs that it may be time to say goodbye:

- Your dog is in pain and no longer responding to treatment.
- Your dog is unable to eat or drink on its own.
- Your dog is unable to control his bodily functions.
- Your dog is no longer able to enjoy life.

The choice of natural death or euthanasia is totally in your hands. Choose what feels right for you, your family, and your Wheaten. If you have questions or doubts, speak with your vet, who will help with your decision. Choosing euthanasia can be very difficult for owners, but ending suffering and pain is also the most compassionate gift we can offer. Understand that euthanasia is painless and quick, done with an overdose of a sedative, literally putting a dog into a deep sleep before his heart stops. If this is your choice, please also make the decision to be with him in his final moments; he will be comforted by the sound of your voice,

Chapter Twelve: Your Aging Wheaten

your gentle hand on his head, and the soothing beat of your heart. Have faith that you have done the right thing and let it go.

Following your dog's death, there are decisions to be made regarding his remains. At-home burials have become illegal in many communities, so you want to check before choosing this method. There are pet cemeteries in some areas, and if this is appealing, you should make arrangements through the cemetery itself. Cremation is the most efficient method of dealing with your pet's remains and can be handled through your veterinarian's office. If you choose to keep your Wheaten's ashes, private cremation must be arranged, also through your veterinarian. Your pet's ashes will be returned to you, usually in a thoughtful container, several days later. Pet cremation urns and charming keepsake receptacles are available online, and there are glass-blowing artisans who will take some of your pet's ashes and encase them in a charming bauble or piece of art.

Grieving

There is nothing abnormal about grieving the loss of your beloved dog. He was an important part of your family—your constant companion and closest confidant. The loss often feels irreparable and unbearable, as though you may never heal from the pain. Don't ever let anyone say to you, "But it's only a dog." Give yourself the grace to heal and permission to mourn and understand that recovering from this loss takes time. Never feel apologetic, and don't ever feel embarrassed to seek help if you are having an especially hard time. Rest assured that you will feel whole again, and when the time is right, you may decide once again to invite a Soft Coated Wheaten Terrier puppy to share your home, hearth, and heart.

Printed in Great Britain
by Amazon